DATE DUE

DE 9'98 NO 18 08			
MR 18 '99			
MY 27 '99			
AG 3'99			
JUL 2 2 '99			
DE 3'99			
AP 13 '00			
DE 4'00			
DE20'00			
JA08'01			
DE 19'01			
JE 5'02			
DE 4'02			
DE17'02			

CRIMINAL JUSTICE

OPPOSING VIEWPOINTS®

OTHER BOOKS OF RELATED INTEREST

OPPOSING VIEWPOINTS SERIES
America's Prisons
Crime and Criminals
The Death Penalty
Gangs
Gun Control
Juvenile Crime
The Legal System
Sexual Violence
Violence
The War on Drugs

CURRENT CONTROVERSIES SERIES
Crime
Drug Trafficking
Gun Control
Hate Crimes
Illegal Drugs
Police Brutality
Violence Against Women
Youth Violence

AT ISSUE SERIES
Date Rape
Does Capital Punishment Deter Crime?
Domestic Violence
The Jury System
Legalizing Drugs
Policing the Police
Rape on Campus

CRIMINAL JUSTICE

OPPOSING VIEWPOINTS®

David L. Bender, *Publisher*
Bruno Leone, *Executive Editor*
Bonnie Szumski, *Editorial Director*
Brenda Stalcup, *Managing Editor*
Scott Barbour, *Senior Editor*
Jill Karson, *Book Editor*

OPPOSING
VIEWPOINTS®
SERIES

Greenhaven Press, Inc., San Diego, California

Cover photo: Photodisc

Library of Congress Cataloging-in-Publication Data

Criminal justice : opposing viewpoints / Jill Karson, book editor.
    p.   cm. — (Opposing viewpoints series)
    Includes bibliographical references (p.   ) and index.
    ISBN 1-56510-795-0 (lib. : alk. paper). —
 ISBN 1-56510-794-2 (pbk. : alk. paper)
    1. Criminal justice, Administration of—Moral and ethical
aspects—United States. I. Karson, Jill. II. Series: Opposing viewpoints
series (Unnumbered)
HV9950.C7445 1998
364.973—dc21   98-4778
                                                                CIP

Greenhaven Press, Inc., P.O. Box 289009
San Diego, CA 92198-9009

"CONGRESS SHALL MAKE NO LAW...ABRIDGING THE FREEDOM OF SPEECH, OR OF THE PRESS."

First Amendment to the U.S. Constitution

The basic foundation of our democracy is the First Amendment guarantee of freedom of expression. The Opposing Viewpoints Series is dedicated to the concept of this basic freedom and the idea that it is more important to practice it than to enshrine it.

CONTENTS

Why Consider Opposing Viewpoints?   9

Introduction   13

Chapter 1: What Reforms Would Improve the Criminal Justice System?

Chapter Preface   16

1. Reforms to Eliminate Racism Are Necessary   17
   Jimmy Carter

2. Reforms to Eliminate Racism Are Not Necessary   21
   Linda Chavez and Robert Lerner

3. The Criminal Justice System Should Focus on
   Rehabilitation   25
   Alan Orfi

4. The Criminal Justice System Should Focus on
   Punishment   29
   Charles H. Logan

5. Reforming the Jury System Would Improve the
   Criminal Justice System   33
   Akhil Reed Amar and Vikram David Amar

6. Many Reforms Are Needed to Improve the
   Criminal Justice System   43
   Ted Gest

7. The Death Penalty Should Be Eliminated   49
   James McCloskey

8. The Death Penalty Should Not Be Eliminated   56
   John Douglas

Periodical Bibliography   63

Chapter 2: Do the Rights of the Accused Undermine the Criminal Justice System?

Chapter Preface   65

1. The Rights of the Accused Must Be Zealously
   Protected   66
   Sol Wachtler

2. Zealous Protection of the Rights of the Accused
   Weakens the Criminal Justice System   71
   Daniel Lungren

3. The *Miranda* Rule Undermines the Criminal
   Justice System   76
   Paul Cassell and Stephen J. Markman

4. The *Miranda* Rule Does Not Undermine the
   Criminal Justice System   84
   Susan R. Klein

5. The Exclusionary Rule Weakens the Criminal
   Justice System   90
   Morgan O. Reynolds

6. The Exclusionary Rule Is Necessary   94
   Carol S. Steiker

Periodical Bibliography   99

**Chapter 3: What Sentencing Laws Should Guide
the Criminal Justice System?**

Chapter Preface   101

1. "Three Strikes" Laws Can Reduce Crime   103
   David LaCourse Jr.

2. "Three Strikes" Laws Are Inconsistent and
   Overly Punitive   109
   Joseph D. McNamara

3. Mandatory Minimum Sentencing Should
   Be Abolished   114
   Vincent L. Broderick

4. Mandatory Minimum Sentencing Is Necessary   122
   Jay Apperson

5. States Should Adopt Truth-in-Sentencing Laws   128
   James Wootton

6. States Should Not Adopt Truth-in-Sentencing Laws   138
   Marc Mauer

Periodical Bibliography   148

**Chapter 4: How Does the Legal System Affect
Criminal Justice?**

Chapter Preface   150

1. The Criminal Trial Is Too Adversarial   151
   Franklin Strier

2. The Criminal Trial Should Be More Adversarial   159
   Kenneth B. Nunn

3. A Case for Defending the Guilty   165
   Robert L. Shapiro

4. A Case for Not Defending the Guilty   172
   Vincent Bugliosi
5. Defense Attorneys Distort the Truth   177
   Harold J. Rothwax
6. Defense Attorneys Do Not Distort the Truth   185
   Charles M. Sevilla
Periodical Bibliography   192

For Further Discussion   193
Organizations to Contact   196
Bibliography of Books   200
Index   203

WHY CONSIDER OPPOSING VIEWPOINTS?

"The only way in which a human being can make some approach to knowing the whole of a subject is by hearing what can be said about it by persons of every variety of opinion and studying all modes in which it can be looked at by every character of mind. No wise man ever acquired his wisdom in any mode but this."

John Stuart Mill

In our media-intensive culture it is not difficult to find differing opinions. Thousands of newspapers and magazines and dozens of radio and television talk shows resound with differing points of view. The difficulty lies in deciding which opinion to agree with and which "experts" seem the most credible. The more inundated we become with differing opinions and claims, the more essential it is to hone critical reading and thinking skills to evaluate these ideas. Opposing Viewpoints books address this problem directly by presenting stimulating debates that can be used to enhance and teach these skills. The varied opinions contained in each book examine many different aspects of a single issue. While examining these conveniently edited opposing views, readers can develop critical thinking skills such as the ability to compare and contrast authors' credibility, facts, argumentation styles, use of persuasive techniques, and other stylistic tools. In short, the Opposing Viewpoints Series is an ideal way to attain the higher-level thinking and reading skills so essential in a culture of diverse and contradictory opinions.

In addition to providing a tool for critical thinking, Opposing Viewpoints books challenge readers to question their own strongly held opinions and assumptions. Most people form their opinions on the basis of upbringing, peer pressure, and personal, cultural, or professional bias. By reading carefully balanced opposing views, readers must directly confront new ideas as well as the opinions of those with whom they disagree. This is not to simplistically argue that everyone who reads opposing views will—or should—change his or her opinion. Instead, the series enhances readers' understanding of their own views by encouraging confrontation with opposing ideas. Careful examination of others' views can lead to the readers' understanding of the logical inconsistencies in their own opinions, perspective on why they hold an opinion, and the consideration of the possibility that their opinion requires further evaluation.

EVALUATING OTHER OPINIONS

To ensure that this type of examination occurs, Opposing Viewpoints books present all types of opinions. Prominent spokespeople on different sides of each issue as well as well-known professionals from many disciplines challenge the reader. An additional goal of the series is to provide a forum for other, less known, or even unpopular viewpoints. The opinion of an ordinary person who has had to make the decision to cut off life support from a terminally ill relative, for example, may be just as valuable and provide just as much insight as a medical ethicist's professional opinion. The editors have two additional purposes in including these less known views. One, the editors encourage readers to respect others' opinions—even when not enhanced by professional credibility. It is only by reading or listening to and objectively evaluating others' ideas that one can determine whether they are worthy of consideration. Two, the inclusion of such viewpoints encourages the important critical thinking skill of objectively evaluating an author's credentials and bias. This evaluation will illuminate an author's reasons for taking a particular stance on an issue and will aid in readers' evaluation of the author's ideas.

As series editors of the Opposing Viewpoints Series, it is our hope that these books will give readers a deeper understanding of the issues debated and an appreciation of the complexity of even seemingly simple issues when good and honest people disagree. This awareness is particularly important in a democratic society such as ours in which people enter into public debate to determine the common good. Those with whom one disagrees should not be regarded as enemies but rather as people whose views deserve careful examination and may shed light on one's own.

Thomas Jefferson once said that "difference of opinion leads to inquiry, and inquiry to truth." Jefferson, a broadly educated man, argued that "if a nation expects to be ignorant and free . . . it expects what never was and never will be." As individuals and as a nation, it is imperative that we consider the opinions of others and examine them with skill and discernment. The Opposing Viewpoints Series is intended to help readers achieve this goal.

David L. Bender & Bruno Leone,
Series Editors

Greenhaven Press anthologies primarily consist of previously published material taken from a variety of sources, including periodicals, books, scholarly journals, newspapers, government documents, and position papers from private and public organizations. These original sources are often edited for length and to ensure their accessibility for a young adult audience. The anthology editors also change the original titles of these works in order to clearly present the main thesis of each viewpoint and to explicitly indicate the opinion presented in the viewpoint. These alterations are made in consideration of both the reading and comprehension levels of a young adult audience. Every effort is made to ensure that Greenhaven Press accurately reflects the original intent of the authors included in this anthology.

INTRODUCTION

"The criminal law is where society and the individual meet as adversaries—with liberty and even life at stake."
—Judge Harold J. Rothwax

America's trials are based on the adversary system, which seeks justice by requiring two opposing lawyers—the prosecutor and defense attorney—to face each other in court and argue their case to the best of their ability. In theory, the clash of opposing views meted out by sophisticated, evenly matched attorneys will reveal truth in the courtroom, yielding the fairest trial possible.

While most people embrace the notion that every person is entitled to a fair trial, a growing faction of Americans is concerned that despite all of its lofty principles, the adversarial trial court does not dispense justice. These critics charge that the trial has become a game dominated by a sporting match mentality, in which winning becomes the sole goal and truth is the casualty. While attorneys are indeed obligated to represent their clients zealously within the bounds of the law, critics argue, the canon of legal ethics allows lawyers boundaries so extraordinarily wide that dishonesty is rampant. As attorney Floyd Abrams noted, "Whether my client was guilty or not, whether I suspected he was guilty or not, I was obliged to defend him. But you are not obliged to believe me when I do so."

Recent high-profile criminal cases have added fuel to the growing perception that the adversarial system allows attorneys to evade the truth and brazenly employ tactics calculated to mask the facts of a case. The most pointed example is the 1995 case of O.J. Simpson, who—with the help of a high-priced team of attorneys—was acquitted of charges that he killed his wife and her friend, despite what many believe to be convincing evidence pointing to his guilt. To some, this case demonstrated that a lawyer's only goal is to advance any exculpatory rationalization to fool the jurors and acquit the client. In his book *The Advocate's Devil*, Alan M. Dershowitz remarked: "In this game, there's only one bottom line—winning—whether the client is black or white, guilty or innocent."

Those who indict the system contend that such deficiencies are inherent in a system that rewards lawyers for winning. Yet calls for reform will surely continue to be tempered by those who staunchly defend a system that boasts, in the words of John

Adams, "better that ten guilty go free rather than one innocent should suffer."

Most Americans support the adversarial system of justice, even though many are skeptical of lawyers and the trial process. What reforms, if any, should be made to the system are discussed throughout *Criminal Justice: Opposing Viewpoints*. The topics debated are: What Reforms Would Improve the Criminal Justice System? Do the Rights of the Accused Undermine the Criminal Justice System? What Sentencing Laws Should Guide the Criminal Justice System? How Does the Legal System Affect Criminal Justice? As readers examine the proposals for criminal justice reform and ponder their merit, it might be useful to consider the point made by former Supreme Court Justice Louis Brandeis, "Nearly all legislation involves a weighing of public needs as against private desires; and likewise a weighing of relative social values."

CHAPTER 1

WHAT REFORMS WOULD IMPROVE THE CRIMINAL JUSTICE SYSTEM?

CHAPTER PREFACE

In assessing the defects and deficits of the criminal justice system—and how to fix them—some topics are timeless. For example, whether the death penalty is moral is a centuries-old question, yet one that is still fueled by strong opinions. Historically, every society has wrestled with the problem of punishing and incapacitating its most dangerous criminals in a way that is just and humane. In recent years—since the1970s—support for the death penalty has gained momentum. In the United States today, thirty-eight states use the death penalty as the ultimate sanction against society's worst offenders.

Opponents of the death penalty argue that taking a human life—even that of a heinous murderer—is morally reprehensible and that no one, including the state, has that right. *U.S. News & World Report* columnist Mathew Miller echoes the views of many when he remarks: "When the state officially kills a human being, it abrogates a right of final judgment that is not ours to render."

Death penalty advocates believe that executing murderers is not only an effective tool in the fight against crime, but also a moral statement: By killing murderers, society paradoxically reinforces the sanctity of life. As Princeton professor John J. DiIulio Jr. notes: "Americans value the death penalty not just for its utility as a crime-reduction tool; they value it as a way of doing justice."

Whether the death penalty is immoral—and whether eliminating it would strengthen or hinder justice—is among the topics debated in the following chapter.

> "Many ... minority Americans are convinced, with good reason, that the basic system of justice and law enforcement is not fair."

REFORMS TO ELIMINATE RACISM ARE NECESSARY

Jimmy Carter

Jimmy Carter formerly served as the governor of Georgia and the president of the United States. In the following viewpoint, Carter argues that the criminal justice system is discriminatory against blacks and other minorities, including the poor. Although Carter concedes that much of this bias arises from broader social forces, he charges that politicians pandering to a fear of crime have contributed to the problem, spurring policies that intensify the racial disparity in the criminal justice system. Reformers should work to implement strategies to target racism and ensure a fair and effective system of justice, he concludes.

As you read, consider the following questions:

1. According to the author, what reforms improved the justice system in the 1970s?
2. In Carter's opinion, why is the sentence imposed for the possession of crack racist?
3. According to Carter, in what way have punishments become overly punitive?

Reprinted from Jimmy Carter, "Rid the Justice System of Racism," *Los Angeles Times*, November 2, 1995, by permission of the Los Angeles Times, ©1995.

American society is steadily becoming more racially and economically polarized. Many poor and minority Americans are convinced, with good reason, that the basic system of justice and law enforcement is not fair.

When my three sons were in college, I realized that they were experimenting with marijuana. This was of great concern to me, but I was confident that an arrest would not destroy their lives.

Ours was a prominent family. I knew the sheriff and judge well, and we could deliver valuable political support on election days. I always felt that they would not want to send "one of the Carter boys" to the state penitentiary. My promise to enroll them in a military school or to guarantee their future good behavior would have substituted for prison.

I also realized, subliminally, that if arrested on the same charge, our African-American neighbors would not have fared so well.

Separate but Equal

This was the era when even the most distinguished lawyers (including a majority of U.S. Supreme Court justices) maintained that "separate but equal" should be the law of the land. Most church leaders proved, through selective Bible verses, that God had ordained the superiority of whites.

Yet during the early 1970s, reacting against segregation, there was a common desire—even competition—among us state governors to reform the system.

With Georgia's enlightened prison director, Dr. Ellis Mac-Dougall, I visited the penitentiaries. We found abominable conditions. Almost invariably, the inmates were poor, most were black and 35% were mentally retarded.

We uncovered many cases of convictions on false accusations, trials with inadequate or almost nonexistent legal counsel and confessions obtained under duress or with false promises of leniency. There was an unwholesome traffic in pardons and paroles by some lawyers and even state legislators who had no legal training. They would charge relatively ignorant family members exorbitant monthly fees in return for helping to obtain what were actually routine paroles of penitentiary inmates.

Reforms

We established early-release and work-release programs. I recruited and helped train volunteer probation officers from service organizations. We gave thorough examinations to all incoming inmates to determine their existing and potential skills. We helped each plan a career for the years in prison and after release.

Many governors embraced this approach, and it resulted in a substantial reduction in the number of prisoners. There were no executions in any states.

RACISM IN THE CRIMINAL JUSTICE SYSTEM

The key findings of [a report released by the Sentencing Project in October 1995] are the following:

• Almost one in three (32.2%) young black men in the age group 20–29 is under criminal justice supervision on any given day—in prison or jail, on probation or parole.

• The cost of criminal justice control for these 827,440 young African American males is about $6 billion a year.

• In recent years, African American women have experienced the greatest increase in criminal justice supervision of all demographic groups, with their rate of criminal justice supervision rising by 78% from 1989–94.

• Drug policies constitute the single most significant factor contributing to the rise in criminal justice populations in recent years, with the number of incarcerated drug offenders having risen by 510% from 1983 to 1993. The number of Black (non-Hispanic) women incarcerated in state prisons for drug offenses increased more than eight-fold—828%—from 1986 to 1991.

• While African American arrest rates for violent crime—45% of arrests nationally—are disproportionate to their share of the population, this proportion has not changed significantly for twenty years. For drug offenses, though, the African American proportion of arrests increased from 24% in 1980 to 39% in 1993, well above the African American proportion of drug users nationally.

• African Americans and Hispanics constitute almost 90% of offenders sentenced to state prison for drug possession.

Marc Mauer and Tracey Huling, *The Sentencing Project*, October 1995.

Has the situation improved since then? Definitely not.

In fact, we've gotten away from the concepts of societal forgiveness and reconciliation. The days of prison reform and rehabilitation of inmates are gone.

THE VOGUE FOR HARSH PUNISHMENT

Now one of the most effective campaign themes among political demagogues is the harshness of their treatment of offenders. It is more popular for a governor to boast of the prison cells built than of new schoolrooms.

The range of capital crimes has skyrocketed at the state and federal level, and death penalties are executed with a literal vengeance.

America now has the highest proportion of its citizens in jail of any country on Earth.

One of the most dramatic changes, initiated in California, is "three strikes and you're out," which eliminates any possibility of freedom for a repeat felon. My own state government trumped this by imposing "two strikes and you're out," and the governor is now attempting to limit exercise and similar "privileges" for prisoners.

Once again, shackled prisoners are working alongside the roads in Alabama, and visitors who stop to enjoy the sight can buy "chain gang" hats and other souvenirs.

These changes have been made because harsh treatment is popular with voters, but there is no indication that it deters crime.

With little chance for rehabilitation, hopelessness prevails in the prisons where the rising sense of injustice and despair has led to an epidemic of revolts.

RACIST POLICIES

Deliberately or not, punishments are focused on black offenders. For instance, sentences for possession or sale of crack cocaine are much more severe than for the chemically identical powder cocaine used by wealthy addicts.

This is not just an accident. In October 1995, Congress reconsidered this inequity and refused to amend the 1986 crack cocaine law, which is applied among blacks 22 times more often than whites.

There is a strong element of discrimination here, based on race and poverty. This is a troubling example of how the attitude and standards of a society can be modified by prejudice.

Nowadays, the Old Testament standard of just one "eye for an eye" is not harsh enough. In Biblical times, it was considered progressive: one eye for a lost eye, so the punishment could not exceed the crime. Today, in many cases, the punishment for some offenders far exceeds the injury resulting from the crime.

As was the case when racial segregation was the law, it is time for America's legal system to correct itself.

Unfortunately, reform voices are muted.

| "Black defendants actually have a better chance of escaping conviction than do white defendants."

REFORMS TO ELIMINATE RACISM ARE NOT NECESSARY

Linda Chavez and Robert Lerner

Linda Chavez is the president of the Center for Equal Opportunity in Washington, D.C. Robert Lerner, the president of Lerner and Nagai Quantitative Consulting in Rockville, Maryland, conducted a study for the center that suggests that blacks are more likely than whites to escape conviction. In the following viewpoint, Chavez and Lerner argue that the results of the study debunk the notion that the criminal justice system is rigged against blacks. They maintain that even if there is some racism in the system—such as racist cops eager to charge blacks with crimes they did not commit—the fact that so many black defendants are cleared proves that the system works in favor of blacks.

As you read, consider the following questions:

1. According to the authors, what two types of felonies result in higher conviction rates for blacks?
2. According to Chavez and Lerner, in what way might the behavior of juries create a trickle-down effect that protects blacks?
3. How might those who believe the justice system is racist explain the higher rate of nonconviction among blacks, in the authors' opinion?

From Linda Chavez and Robert Lerner, "Is the Justice System Rigged Against Blacks?" *Wall Street Journal*, December 4, 1996. Reprinted with permission of the *Wall Street Journal*, ©1996 Dow Jones & Company, Inc. All rights reserved.

Nearly 100 years ago W.E.B. Du Bois warned, "the Negro is coming more and more to look upon law and justice, not as protecting safeguards but as sources of humiliation and oppression." Little apparently has changed since then. A recent Gallup poll showed that nearly two-thirds of blacks believe that the criminal justice system is rigged against them.

Many civil rights advocacy groups agree, pointing to harsher penalties for black crack offenders than for white cocaine dealers and to allegedly higher death penalty rates for blacks.

George Washington University law professor Paul Butler, who is a former federal prosecutor, has suggested the remedy ought to be widespread jury nullification. [Jury nullification occurs when juries that disagree with the law or the law's application acquit guilty defendants.] "It is, in fact, the moral responsibility of black jurors to emancipate some guilty black outlaws," he wrote in the *Yale Law Journal* in 1995.

But does the justice system really discriminate against blacks? Before anyone follows Prof. Butler's advice it would be useful to look at what hard data tell us about the conviction rates of blacks and whites. The Center for Equal Opportunity has released a study showing that black defendants actually have a better chance of escaping conviction than do white defendants. Although most non-convictions come through dismissal, dismissal with plea to a lesser charge, or a not guilty finding by a judge, the report also suggests that blacks are more likely to be acquitted when their trials go to jury.

BLACK AND WHITE CONVICTION RATES

The study was based upon data compiled by the Bureau of Justice Statistics from more than 55,000 state felony cases filed in the 75 largest counties in May 1992. (See the nearby table.) It looked at 14 different kinds of felonies. In only two of them— felony traffic offenses and a catchall category called "other felonies"— were blacks more likely than whites to receive a conviction. In the other 12, white defendants were more likely than blacks to earn punishment. These categories included the crimes of murder, rape, robbery, assault, burglary, drug trafficking and weapons charges. They accounted for more than 98% of the crimes examined.

The differences between black and white conviction rates were often close. Although 24% of black defendants charged with murder had their cases either acquitted or dismissed, 23% of whites also escaped conviction. For robbery, the rates were 38% and 35%, respectively. For assault, they were 49% and 43%.

But in some areas the differences were quite large. A majority of black defendants—51%—charged with rape were either acquitted or saw the charges dismissed. Yet only one-quarter of whites could make the same claim. In another category of crime that includes child abuse, extortion and manslaughter (the Bureau of Justice Statistics calls these "other crimes against persons"), blacks beat the rap 48% of the time vs. 28% for whites.

Who Beats the Rap?

Non-convictions (dismissals and acquittals) by race

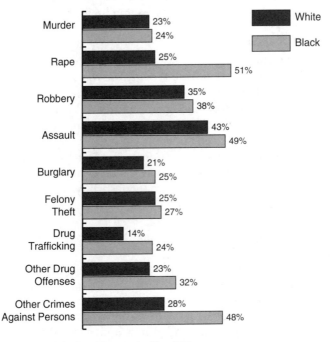

Source: Center for Equal Opportunity, May 1992

Linda Chavez and Robert Lerner, *Wall Street Journal*, December 4, 1996.

Fewer than 3% of the cases examined actually went before a jury. Because of this small number, it is unwise to draw sweeping conclusions about the behavior of juries from this sample. Yet the verdicts do lend credence to the claim that blacks are more likely than whites to avoid conviction. An astonishing 83% of black defendants charged with rape were acquitted, compared with only 24% of whites. Blacks were also more likely to be acquitted by juries when they were charged with murder, burglary, felony theft, drug trafficking and other crimes against persons. Whites had somewhat better odds at acquittal when charged with robbery and assault.

The fact that few cases go before a jury should not diminish their importance. The behavior of juries creates a trickle-down effect that touches defendants throughout the criminal justice pipeline. If prosecutors believe that juries are likely to approach certain kinds of cases with a bias, they may be more or less likely to drop a case or offer a plea-bargain prior to an actual courtroom trial. In other words, if black defendants stand a good chance of being acquitted by a jury, they may face more lenient treatment in all the stages leading up to that moment.

A RACIAL CONSPIRACY?

Those who subscribe to the notion of a racist conspiracy in the criminal justice system have a ready answer to explain these numbers. The higher rate of non-conviction among blacks, they say, is a direct result of having over-charged them with crimes they did not commit. . . . Racist cops are eager to throw the book at blacks, so they charge innocent persons.

If this were true—and the Center for Equal Opportunity's study sheds no light on this issue—the data show plenty of defendants are ultimately cleared by the justice system, suggesting the system has built-in safeguards that prevent racism from running its full course.

There is another way to interpret the data, of course. Some jurors may very well be engaging in race-based nullification, just as Prof. Butler advocates. Although the nationwide acquittal rate is reported to be between 15% and 20%, it can go much higher in urban areas with large black populations and a high percentage of black defendants. In Washington, D.C., nearly one-quarter of all felony trials ended in acquittals in 1995. "I have seen race become more of an issue, and it has resulted in more acquittals and hung juries," D.C. Superior Court Judge Reggie B. Walton told *Reader's Digest* in June 1996. In the Bronx, almost half of all minority defendants in felony cases go free.

If so, a different kind of racism is at play, not one where the deck is stacked against black defendants.

| "The problem with the punitive approach to criminal justice is that it can debilitate prisoners rather than 'correct' them."

THE CRIMINAL JUSTICE SYSTEM SHOULD FOCUS ON REHABILITATION

Alan Orfi

Alan Orfi is an inmate at a correctional facility in Minnesota and the editor of *Prison Mirror*, a monthly periodical that explores issues germane to prisoners. In the following viewpoint, Orfi argues that prison life entails great pain and suffering. The long-term effect of such a punitive atmosphere, he charges, is debilitating to prisoners and increases the risk of recidivism. Because most inmates will eventually return to society, Orfi insists, rehabilitation is a smarter option. By focusing on helping inmates instead of punishing them, he concludes, the criminal justice system will produce citizens who are able to successfully re-enter society.

As you read, consider the following questions:

1. What factors contribute to recidivism, according to Orfi?
2. What are some of the reasons that the public supports "get tough" policies, in Orfi's opinion?
3. According to the author, what percentage of prisoners return to society?

Reprinted, with permission, from Alan Orfi, "The Pain of Prison," *Prison Mirror*, April 1, 1995.

I have been down for only two and a half years, but, as I look back and reflect upon this experience, I realize just how misguided my preconceived notions about incarceration were. I expected prison life to be wrought with violence and mayhem, but I discovered right away that most inmates are just like the people you run into every day on the streets. Contrary to media portrayals of inmates in general, I have found most prisoners (at least at this correctional facility) to be honest, committed to their families, and generally caring of others. In fact, I have developed more meaningful friendships with people here than I ever did on the outside.

However, one thing that I underestimated was the amount of pain that prison life entails. The mental anguish and despair prisoners endure on a daily basis can be overwhelming. Visitors to the prison can see our cells with our television sets and basic amenities and leave the institution thinking that conditions are not all that harsh. However, they do not see the real pain of our prison life which lies within its relentless monotony and isolation, the utter wastefulness of our unproductive time in here and the agony of being away from our loved ones for so long. The wife of an Oak Park Heights inmate told *The Perspective* in April 1994 that she found it impossible to look back at her husband after they had said their goodbyes. She said, "I did it once and the look on his face scared me. His features were twisted into an unrecognizable mask." This is the type of pain that prisoners endure daily and its long-term effect is devastating.

"GET TOUGH" POLICIES

Despite the fact that overall crime rates have remained virtually steady since 1980, American citizens have been calling for more punitive means of criminal justice. Consequently, this nation has supported dramatic increases in the lengths of sentences, the readoption of the death penalty and a concentrated effort put forth by corrections officials to implement more "punitive" living conditions for prisoners. Prisons are getting tougher again.

This retaliatory approach to criminal justice appears to help the general public feel that they are at least doing something to combat crime. Politicians have been more than willing to jump on the "get tough" bandwagon. We all heard Minnesota Governor Arne Carlson repeatedly tell voters during his re-election campaign in the fall of 1994 that "criminals are in prison to be punished." If you are a politician today, you really can't say that enough.

The problem with the punitive approach to criminal justice is that it can debilitate prisoners rather than "correct" them.

Inmates often leave prison having lost their families, their homes, their money, their dignity, and now possess a criminal record which will greatly hinder their efforts to gain meaningful employment. These are only the more obvious factors in the high rate of recidivism amongst released inmates.

A Case for Rehabilitation

No empirical evidence has been found linking punishment with a reduction in crime.

The public's desire for safety, as opposed to punishment, is swinging corrections back toward the goal of providing meaningful interventions that change offenders' behavior. Strong public support exists for programs that return offenders to society as law-abiding citizens.

Successful interventions include the use of community resources for meeting individual needs, family therapy, diversion and treatment for substance abuse or sexual deviation. Effective programs also take into account the issue of risk—the higher the potential for criminal activity by the offender, the greater the intervention must be.

Dave Dillingham, *Corrections Today*, February 1994.

The systematic debilitation of prison inmates is something which receives virtually little attention, yet plays an enormous role in the problem of crime in America. A person subjected to pain and isolation for a long period of time learns to develop coping mechanisms which may make re-entry into society very difficult. The harshness of the prison environment can cause an inmate to adopt survival strategies that, in actuality, render him a much more dangerous person than he was before he entered the system. Lengthy separations from the loved ones who give stability and meaning to a person's life can cause an agony which time may not heal. This kind of pain is debilitating and it does nothing to make a convicted person a better citizen.

REHABILITATION AND RECIDIVISM

It is clear that crime is a very serious problem, but it is also equally alarming to watch societal attitudes grow more retaliatory in nature. The common theme amongst the hard-liners is that prisoners have it too easy in prison and that they don't deserve such "luxuries" as phone privileges, televisions or opportunities for furthering their education. But once that person gets past their eye-for-an-eye mentality, they might realize that the issue is not about *deserving* anything. The issue is about *crime*—and the rehabilitation of those who have committed crimes. The question of whether or not inmates deserve certain privileges needs to be put aside so that the issues of rehabilitation and recidivism can be addressed. Warden Benson told the *Twin Cities Reader* in 1993 that some of the pressure he receives is derived from a societal misunderstanding of these issues. He said, "People hear about rehabilitation. They hear the convicts can get a college education, and they think we're coddling them. Well, practically speaking, these people are going to be your neighbors when they get out—they're going to sit next to you on the bus."

This is the most pertinent fact that society is forgetting in their outcry for longer and more severe punishments. The bottom line is that 98% of all inmates will eventually return to society. Like any person, a prison inmate is very likely to become a product of his environment and the fact is that, even in 1995, prison life is very difficult. This current trend of making prisons even more punitive serves only the purpose of further debilitating people who already face an uphill battle when the time comes for them to re-enter society. With regard to recidivism, the "get tough" policy is not only ineffective, it is just plain dangerous.

> "Punishment through imprisonment is above all else an expression of our sense of justice and of the value our society places on freedom and on individual responsibility."

THE CRIMINAL JUSTICE SYSTEM SHOULD FOCUS ON PUNISHMENT

Charles H. Logan

In the following viewpoint, Charles H. Logan argues that the criminal justice system must send a clarion call to prisoners and would-be criminals: Those who commit felonies will be punished. Logan contends that this vital message becomes blurred when the penal system attempts to rehabilitate offenders. Implicit in the mission of rehabilitation, he maintains, is the notion that criminals are victims of social and personal deficiencies beyond their control. In his view, the system should instead stress personal accountability, an approach that would not excuse or encourage crime. Logan is a professor of sociology at the University of Connecticut and the author of *Private Prisons: Cons and Pros*.

As you read, consider the following questions:

1. According to the author, what prompts positive reform of criminal behavior?
2. In Logan's opinion, how might rehabilitation actually encourage crime?
3. What are the benefits of prison privatization, according to Logan?

Reprinted from Charles H. Logan, "Run Prisons Differently," *American Enterprise*, May/June 1995, by permission of the *American Enterprise*, a Washington, D.C.–based magazine of politics, business, and culture.

Prisons are the favorite whipping boy of every critic of the American criminal justice system. Some say we have too many of them, others too few. It is argued that prisons are too full, that they cost too much, that they have become too comfortable, or not comfortable enough. There are questions as to whether they rehabilitate, deter, or even incapacitate.

Some of these controversies would clear up if we had a better understanding of the practical and moral importance of prisons. Punishment through imprisonment is above all else an expression of our sense of justice and of the value our society places on freedom and on individual responsibility. Doing justice is the true mission of our prisons, and the single most important thing we can do to aid them is to purge them of any official responsibility for rehabilitation.

Prisons should not try to be "correctional institutions." Changing behavior is not impossible—the majority of those released from prison do not return—but it happens only through self-restraint and individual reform. When we define rehabilitation as a collective responsibility to be achieved through the criminal justice system, the principle of accountability gets blurred.

THE MESSAGE OF IMPRISONMENT

The message of prison should be simple: "Felonies are wrong and controllable acts, and those who commit them will be punished." Institutions aiming for "rehabilitation" more often transmit this muddled message: "Felonies are the result of social and personal deficiencies (of opportunity, knowledge, skills, habits, temperament, and so on), and society has a responsibility to correct those deficiencies." That message depicts criminal behavior as uncontrollable rather than willful, and portrays offenders as automatons in need of adjustment rather than responsible human beings who must accept the consequences of their actions. Such a message may excuse, and even encourage, crime; at the very least, it weakens the vital punishment message of imprisonment.

"But," we are warned, "most prisoners will return to society eventually; don't we want them to come back prepared to lead noncriminal lives?" Indeed, we do. We not only want that, we demand it—but we demand it of the victimizer, not of the prison system. And in this we do not ask much: Do not hit, rob, rape, kill, swindle, or otherwise aggress against your fellow citizens. Those whom we send to prison, rather than to a mental hospital, already have all the equipment they need to refrain from crime. What they do with their lives beyond that is not the business of the penal system.

PUNISHMENT WORKS

Scholarly studies say rehabilitation programs just don't work. RAND [a nonprofit research institution] researchers reported recently on a controlled experiment in which the experimental group of criminals received far more treatment services than a control group. But a one-year follow-up found no differences in arrests or self-admitted crime between the two groups. A well publicized Community Corrections Partnership in Cincinnati labored mightily to boost the "self-esteem" and "sense of community" of black teen-age felons on probation. But the same percentage of this group were rearrested as in the comparable group on regular probation. Perhaps Ralph Adam Fine, a circuit court judge on the Wisconsin Court of Appeals in Milwaukee, said it best: "We keep our hands out of a flame because it hurt the very first time (not the second, fifth or 10th time) we touched fire." We have an unpleasant method of dealing with crime—punishment and deterrence—that works, and a pleasant method—rehabilitation—that doesn't.

Pete du Pont, *Washington Times*, February 12, 1995.

So, how can we improve the effectiveness of prisons in curbing anti-social behavior and carrying out justice? For one thing, sentences need to be less rubbery. Most prisoners today have committed crimes that average citizens strongly believe should lead to imprisonment, and the specific sentences imposed generally reflect a broad consensus about the seriousness of various crimes. Once handed down, these sentences should be served in their entirety. To convey a clear message about the wrongness of crime, we need a system in which punishments are carried out fully as prescribed. When sentences get reduced sometime after sentencing for expedient reasons we end up with unfairness (as when a murderer ends up doing less time than a thief) and mixed signals to lawbreakers (as when a crime that is declared to deserve 10 years of loss of liberty actually only brings three years. Thus we need truth in sentencing: a requirement that all prisoners serve at least 85 percent of their sentence.

PRISON PRIVATIZATION

To meet the current level of serious crime in the United States we also need more prisons. We can afford this—prisons remain a small, if growing, portion of government spending. But we certainly don't want to waste money on them. How can taxpayers tell if their government is giving them good value for their prison dollars? The best guarantee is to put the government in competition with the private sector.

As of June 1994, there were 84 private prison facilities with a total capacity of 43,508 beds under contract with various government bodies. A growing body of research demonstrates that these private prisons save money, improve quality, and protect inmates' rights, and that they produce no problems not already faced by governmental operations. Prison privatization has been called "controversial," but most of the resistance has been manufactured by dedicated opponents like public employee unions who feel threatened at the prospect of competition (as well they should). A decade of mostly positive experience has proven the value of private prisons.

"If the jury system is to remain a central institution of democracy and citizenship, it must be refined."

REFORMING THE JURY SYSTEM WOULD IMPROVE THE CRIMINAL JUSTICE SYSTEM

Akhil Reed Amar and Vikram David Amar

In the following viewpoint, Akhil Reed Amar and Vikram David Amar outline what they view as shortcomings in the system and suggest a number of key reforms to improve the administration of justice by jury. For example, they maintain that if peremptory strikes were limited, juries would become more representative. They also advocate changes that would increase a jury's ability to evaluate the facts, including allowing jurors to take notes and question witnesses. Akhil Reed Amar is Southmayd Professor of Law at Yale Law School. Vikram David Amar is Acting Professor of Law at the University of California at Davis.

As you read, consider the following questions:

1. Why should peremptory challenges be limited, according to the authors?
2. In the authors' view, what is the benefit of allowing jurors to question the witnesses?
3. According to the authors, what three arguments support their view that nonunanimous verdicts should be upheld?

Reprinted from Akhil Reed Amar and Vikram David Amar, "Unlocking the Jury Box," *Policy Review*, May/June 1996, by permission of the Heritage Foundation.

The Founders of our nation understood that no idea was more central to our Bill of Rights—indeed, to government of the people, by the people, and for the people—than the citizen jury. It was cherished not only as a bulwark against tyranny but also as an essential means of educating Americans in the habits and duties of citizenship. By enacting the Fifth, Sixth, and Seventh Amendments to the Constitution, the Framers sought to install the right to trial by jury as a cornerstone of a free society.

FAILINGS OF THE SYSTEM

Today that cornerstone is crumbling. In recent years, a parade of notorious criminal trials has called into question the value of citizen juries. The prosecutions of Oliver North, O.J. Simpson, William Kennedy Smith, the Menendez brothers, and the assailants of Rodney King and Reginald Denny have made armchair jurors of millions of Americans. Now the failings of the system seem obvious to anyone with a television:

• In search of "impartial" jurors, the selection process seems stacked against the educated, the perceptive, and the well informed in favor of those more easily manipulated by lawyers and judges. Attorneys exercising their rights to strike candidates from the pool cynically and slyly seek to exclude jurors on the basis of race, gender, and other supposed indicators of bias.

• Courts subject citizens to repeated summonses, intrusive personal questioning, and long and inefficient trials. Unsurprisingly, many citizens avoid jury duty.

• In court, jurors serve a passive role dictated by rules that presume jurors are incapable of impartial deliberation and that provide little help in understanding points of law or evaluating testimony.

• The public perceives that the scales of justice tip in favor of rich defendants with high-priced counsel.

More than a million Americans serve as jurors on state courts each year. Jury service offers these Americans an unequaled opportunity to participate democratically in the administration of justice. But on its present course, this vital egalitarian institution may shrivel up, avoided by citizens, manipulated by lawyers and litigants, and ridiculed by the general public. To be sure, the system has inherent limitations; "correct" verdicts cannot be guaranteed. But given the jury's present form, society is bearing the costs of a jury system's vices without enjoying a jury system's virtues. Our task is to demonstrate why the citizen jury is worth defending, and to propose a number of specific reforms designed to restore the jury to its rightful status in a democracy under law.

The Framers of the Constitution felt that juries—because they were composed of ordinary citizens and because they owed no financial allegiance to the government—were indispensable to thwarting the excesses of powerful and overzealous government officials. . . .

The need for juries was especially acute in criminal cases: A grand jury could block any prosecution it deemed unfounded or malicious, and a petit jury could likewise interpose itself on behalf of a defendant charged unfairly. . . .

But the Founders' vision of the jury went far beyond merely protecting defendants. The jury's democratic role was intertwined with other ideas enshrined in the Bill of Rights, including free speech and citizen militias. The jury was an essential democratic institution because it was a means by which citizens could engage in self-government. Nowhere else—not even in the voting booth—must Americans come together in person to deliberate over fundamental matters of justice. Jurors face a solemn obligation to overlook personal differences and prejudices to fairly administer the law and do justice. . . .

Perhaps most important was the jury's educational mission. Through the jury, citizens would learn self-government by doing it. In the words of Alexis de Tocqueville, "The jury is both the most effective way of establishing the people's rule and the most effective way of teaching them how to rule." This learning, of course, would carry over to other political activity. As Tocqueville explained:

"Juries, especially civil juries, instill some of the habits of the judicial mind into every citizen, and just those habits are the very best way of preparing people to be free. . . . They make all men feel that they have duties toward society and that they take a share in its government. By making men pay more attention to things other than their own affairs, they combat that individual selfishness which is like rust in society. . . . [The jury] should be regarded as a free school which is always open and in which each juror learns his rights, . . . and is given practical lessons in the law. . . . I think that the main reason for the . . . political good sense of the Americans is their long experience with juries in civil cases." . . .

JUSTICE'S WEAK LINK?
The weaknesses of jury trials are sometimes ascribed to the mediocre capacity of ordinary citizens to adjudicate matters of law and fact in an increasingly complex society. It is true that jurors will not always decide "correctly," any more than voters

will always choose the most qualified candidates for public office. But the real problem is not that we rely too much on men and women of ordinary intelligence and common sense to decide questions of fact and value in the courtroom. The problem is that we rely too little. The jury is crippled by constraints imposed by the court professionals.

In the era of the Founders, the jury was no more egalitarian than was suffrage, limited by race and sex and by tests of personal traits thought necessary for judging cases. Over two centuries, even as the right of jury service was gradually extended to all citizens of voting age, the freedom of jurors to participate in the finding of fact in the courtroom was constricted. Contrary to the spirit in which the jury trial was woven into our constitutional fabric, judges and lawyers have aggrandized their own roles in litigation at the expense of the jury.

The deepest constitutional function of the jury is to serve not the parties but the people—by involving them in the administration of justice and the grand project of democratic self-government. Alas, over the years, the search for adversarial advantage by attorneys won out over the values of public education and participation.

Judges, charged with protecting these enduring constitutional values, have at times done just the opposite in order to maintain their control over trials. The jury was to check the judge—much as the legislature was to check the executive, the House of Representatives to check the Senate, and the states to check the national government.

It is not surprising that we—as jurors, as citizens—have not fought off these creeping assaults. The benefits of jury service are widely dispersed—they redound to fellow citizens as well as the individual jurors. But the individual juror bears all of the cost—the hassle, the inconvenience, the foregone wages—of jury service.

SUGGESTIONS FOR JURY REFORM

If the jury system is to remain a central institution of democracy and citizenship, it must be refined. Jury trials must attract engaged and thoughtful citizens; the rules of the courts must treat jurors as sovereign, self-governing citizens rather than as children. To this end, we suggest a number of reforms. In many instances, these changes would require no new laws, but merely a willingness on the part of the courts to unleash the common sense of the ordinary citizen.

I. *Respect jurors.* First, we must try to design the system to welcome jurors. All too often they are mistreated by the trial process, forced to wait in cramped and uncomfortable quarters while the judge and lawyers question jury candidates, who are often dismissed from selection without explanation. We should use juries to reconnect citizens with each other and with their government. After serving on a jury, a citizen should, in general, feel better—less cynical, more public-regarding—about our system.

II. *Make juries more representative.* Earlier in the nation's history, juries were impaneled under the elitist principle that only the propertied or the highly educated possessed the habits of citizenship needed to serve well. Now that we know better, it is perverse that professional and literate citizens often are exempted or struck from the jury pool. When juries produce stupid verdicts, it is often because we let interested parties pick stupid jurors in stupid ways. It is a scandal that only those who had never heard of Oliver North were permitted to judge him. Now that we have ceded so much control over trials to the court regulars, this shouldn't come as a surprise—it is akin to letting lobbyists hand-pick candidates for office.

A juror should have an open mind but not an empty mind. We must empower juries in ways that make them more representative and less vulnerable to encroachments of the judicial professionals, without turning them into professionals themselves.

Limit peremptory challenges. By and large, the first 12 persons picked by lottery should form the jury. The jury—and not just the jury pool summoned for each case—should be as representative of the entire community as possible. Peremptory challenges (a device that allows lawyers to remove a specified number of jurors from the panel without having to show "cause") should be eliminated; they allow prosecutors and defense attorneys to manipulate demographics and chisel an unrepresentative panel out of a representative pool. Juries should represent the people, not the parties. . . .

Jury pay. We should pay jurors for their time. Payment at a fair, flat rate will permit a broad cross section of society to serve. Payment is appropriate, for judges and legislators are paid for their time. To decline to compensate citizens for their sacrifice—or to pay them a token $5 per day as is done in many California courts—is in effect to impose a functionally regressive poll tax that penalizes the working poor who want to serve on juries, but who cannot afford the loss of a week's pay. Payment should come from the government, not private employers. All jurors are equal as jurors, and should be paid equally: One person, one vote, one paycheck.

III. *Restore the notion of duty.* Jury service is not only a right, but also a duty. Few of us have militantly insisted that we perform this obligation, just as few of us insisted in the last 30 years that we pay our fair share of the intergenerational tax burden. The *Economist* reports that half of all Californians called for jury duty in the state's criminal courts ignore the summons. Citizens should not escape so easily.

A JURY'S CAPACITY TO ACQUIRE INFORMATION

We trust the jury system, yet in many respects we distrust the jurors. The entire body of principles we call the rules of evidence rests on the assumption that ordinary people are too unsophisticated (or too foolish) to sort out the probable from the improbable and too naive to appreciate that an out-of-court statement not made under oath is less worthy of belief than a witness's testimony in open court. Until the late nineteenth century lack of confidence in the jury's common sense even led to excluding from the witness box the defendant in a criminal case and all parties in civil litigation. The stated reason was that their desire for a favorable outcome would irresistibly produce perjury, as if jurors would be less likely to detect false testimony from a party's lips than from those of an ordinary witness.

Perhaps our anxiety is misplaced. Maybe we should worry less about a jury's inability to spot liars and pay more attention to the way a juror must necessarily acquire information. We expect average untrained people to absorb evidence for days and weeks on subjects entirely foreign to them without explanation, clarification, or even the opportunity to take notes or ask questions. Thus we imagine that they can understand a judge's "instructions on the law," often read to them in a monotone and containing principles that law students take a term to master and whose meaning appellate judges often have palpable difficulty establishing.

Hiller B. Zobel, *American Heritage*, July/August 1995.

Few exemptions. Exemptions from service should be extremely limited: If you are the brother-in-law of the plaintiff, you may be excused; but you may not be excused merely because you happen to read the newspaper or work in a profession. The idea of the jury is rooted in equality; just as all defendants are treated equally before the law, all jurors have equal claims as well as obligations to play a part in the administration of justice. This measure would expand the size of the jury pool, enforce the universality of required service, and raise the average education level of juries.

Yearly service. The Swiss defend their country with a citizen militia that regularly requires a citizen to serve a periodic stint of active service. Similarly, we should ask each citizen to devote, say, one week a year to jury service, depending on the needs of his or her jurisdiction. Each citizen could register in advance for the week that is most convenient, and except for genuine emergencies, citizens should then be obliged to serve when their turn comes. Courts should be willing to provide professional day care or day-care vouchers to enable homemakers to take their turns in this project in collective self-governance.

Enforcing the duty. And how should this obligation be enforced? Progressive fines are probably the best option. If you miss your week, you should pay two weeks' salary. (Flat fines, by contrast, would be functionally regressive and create incentives for highly paid citizens to dodge service.) If for some reason fines didn't work, perhaps we could consider a more radical recoupling of jury service with voting: If you want to opt out of the responsibilities of collective self-government, fine—but you may not then exercise any of its rights. You may choose to be a citizen, with democratic rights and duties, or a subject, ruled by others. On this view, you are not entitled to vote outside juries if you are unwilling to serve and vote inside juries. If you are not willing to engage in regular focused deliberation with a random cross section of fellow voters, you should not be governing the polity, just as you may not vote in the Iowa presidential caucuses unless you attend and hear the arguments of your peers.

Serial jurors. Each jury, once constituted, should be able to try several cases in a row. If you can hear four quick cases in your week a year, so much the better. The grand jury reviews more than one indictment, the judge sits on more than one case, and the legislature may decide more than one issue in a session. The quality of deliberations is likely to improve with practice. The burden of jury service will be more evenly distributed—one week for everyone—and more trials can take place if we get rid of all the wasteful preliminaries like elaborate jury questioning and peremptories. Indeed, perhaps a jury should hear both civil and criminal cases in its week. One week a year will not turn citizens into government bureaucrats, though it will give them regular practice in the art of deliberation and self-government.

IV. *Free jurors to do their jobs.* Juries today are often criticized for reaching foolish decisions. But it's not all their fault. Nothing is more important to fulfilling the democratic aims of jury service—including just outcomes—than active participation by the jurors. Over the years, the court professionals have conspired to strip jurors of their ability to evaluate the facts. Running the courtroom to maximize their own convenience, they have often slighted the jury's legitimate needs to understand its role, the law, and the facts. . . .

Taking notes. Many judges do not allow jurors to take notes. This is idiocy. Judges take notes, grand jurors take notes, legislators take notes—what's going on here? This prohibition is based on the misguided beliefs that note-taking distracts jurors from the testimony and that deliberation would be unfairly dominated by jurors with extensive records. Neither fear outweighs the benefit of giving jurors the means to highlight key evidence and keep track of their impressions, particularly in long trials.

Plain-English instructions. Judges should give the panel, at the outset of a case, the basic elements of the charged offenses—in English, not legalese—so jurors can consider them and check them off in their notebooks as the trial unfolds.

Questioning of witnesses. Jurors should be allowed to question witnesses by passing queries to the judge. This allows jurors to pierce the selective presentation of facts offered by counsel, and it also keeps jurors more attentive to proceedings. Best of all, it would expose any lingering confusion about testimony in the minds of the jurors, giving prosecutors and defense counsel the chance to address these concerns. Consider, for example, the possibility that each of the jurors in the O.J. Simpson trial had a different pet theory of police conspiracy. If each juror could submit questions, prosecutors would have had an opportunity to understand, address, and debunk many of these mutually inconsistent and factually insupportable theories.

Discussion among jurors prior to deliberation. A ban on such discussion assumes that jurors are superhumanly capable of suspending all judgment for days or weeks and that conversation can only contaminate their faculties. Common sense suggests that it is human nature to form provisional judgments; at least by discussing a case prior to deliberation, jurors can test each other's impressions of the evidence and begin to hone their understandings of key points before these points are lost in the rush of the proceedings. Such a reform must, of course, be accompanied by reminders from the judge that jurors may not reach final conclusions about guilt or innocence until they have heard all the evidence.

Support staff. We should allow juries to hire support staff when it is necessary. In a world of increasing complexity and specialization of labor, few can do an important job well without such help. If legislators and judges can have staffs, why not grand juries? We trivialize jurors when we insist that they alone remain trapped in the 18th-century world of generalists. Perhaps every court should hire a permanent staff with undivided loyalty to the jury itself, and subject to "term limits" to prevent the staff from entrenching itself and using the jury to advance its own agenda.

V. *Avoid hung juries.* When hung juries occur, mistrials waste the time and resources of all concerned. They even harm defendants in cases where the jury was leaning toward acquittal, because a mistrial allows a vindictive prosecutor a second bite at the apple. All this brings us to another controversial—and we admit extremely tentative—suggestion. Perhaps, just perhaps, we should move, even in criminal cases, away from unanimity toward majority or supermajority rule on juries. Founding history is relatively clear—a criminal jury had to be unanimous. But this clear understanding was not explicitly inscribed into the Constitution, and the modern Supreme Court has upheld state rules permitting convictions on 10-2 votes. (England today also permits 10-2 verdicts in criminal cases.)

Three arguments support our suggestion that nonunanimous verdicts should be upheld. First, at the Founding unanimity may have drawn its strength from certain metaphysical and religious ideas about Truth that are no longer plausible: to wit, that all real truths would command universal assent. Second, most of our analogies tug toward majority rule—used by legislatures, appellate benches, voters, and grand juries—or supermajority rule: In impeachment proceedings, for example, a two-thirds vote in the Senate is required for conviction.

Last, and most important, all our other suggestions lead the modern American jury system away from its historical reliance on unanimity. At the founding of our nation, unanimity within a jury was nestled in a cluster of other rules that now must fall. In early days, blacks, women, the poor, and the young were excluded from voting and jury service. Peremptory challenges probably made juries even more homogenous. But now that all adult citizens may serve on juries, and we have eliminated all the old undemocratic barriers, preserving unanimity might also be undemocratic, for it would create an extreme minority veto unknown to the Founders. . . .

LET THE CHANGES BEGIN

The vision we have sketched is a demanding one. Yet many states are already taking up the challenge, enacting reforms by statute or by court policy. The court system of New York state is mulling over reforms to make the experience of serving more efficient and convenient for citizens, and many states already have a one-day, one-trial policy. New Jersey and New York in 1995 joined the 25 or so states that eliminate exemptions based on profession. Arizona is the leader in endorsing proposals, such as note-taking and questioning witnesses, to increase jurors' participation in the process. Oregon and Louisiana allow nonunanimous verdicts in some cases, and Arizona allows a jury to ask the lawyers to explain evidence again if it has reached an impasse in deliberations.

But much more needs to be done. Until America's state and federal judicial systems live up to the ideals embedded in their founding documents and learn to trust the capacity of ordinary citizens to dispense justice, a cornerstone of democracy will continue to crumble.

"Clearly, the [criminal justice]
system is broken in fundamental
ways."

MANY REFORMS ARE NEEDED TO IMPROVE THE CRIMINAL JUSTICE SYSTEM

Ted Gest

According to Ted Gest, the criminal justice system is in crisis; with violent crime sweeping the nation, only a fraction of the guilty are convicted of felonies and fewer still end up behind bars. In the following viewpoint, Gest identifies ten problem areas that, in his opinion, constitute the system's fundamental flaws. In his critique, Gest includes overworked police officers, excessive delays in courts, a flawed jury system, and insensitivity to crime victims. Until significant reforms are made, he asserts, the public will continue to distrust the criminal justice system. Gest is a senior editor with *U.S. News & World Report*.

As you read, consider the following questions:

1. According to Gest, what is the biggest problem police officers face?
2. In Gest's opinion, why do suspects receive inadequate legal aid?
3. What constitutes "restorative justice," according to the author?

Reprinted, with permission, from Ted Gest, "The Real Problems in American Justice,"
U.S. News & World Report, October 9, 1995. Copyright 1997, U.S. News & World Report.

The criminal justice system was low on Americans' list of esteemed institutions long before the O.J. Simpson case became a national obsession. A recent survey by *U.S. News* found only 8 percent with a "great deal" of confidence in the courts, and the public routinely complains of excessive costs and delays, as well as laxity in sentencing.

A Flawed System of Justice

Clearly, the system is broken in fundamental ways: Each year, 4.3 million violent crimes are committed, but barely more than 200,000 people are convicted of felonies, and a little over half end up going to prison for more than a year. Here's a rundown of the major flaws:

1. *Police solve too few crimes.* Law enforcers never have had it easy, but their modern success rate is staggeringly low. Only 24 percent of robberies and 13 percent of burglaries are cleared by an arrest. Homicide clearance rates are down from 86 percent in 1970 to 66 percent in 1993. Fewer witnesses are willing to testify against today's armed teens. A larger witness-protection program would help.

But the biggest problem is manpower. Some help is on the way as up to 100,000 community-patrol officers were hired under the 1994 federal anticrime law. And shootings already are falling in some New York City precincts, where more police are returning to the beat to deal with both serious crimes and low-level offenses. But critics warn that local patrols take away from investigative units.

2. *Sleuths lose vital evidence.* Harried police officers inadvertently contaminate key items. Crime laboratories, which do everything from alcohol testing to DNA analysis, can compound the problem. Historically, they have been a low priority for public funds. Technicians often receive scant training, and, until recently, few of the nation's 358 labs worked under any quality control. But quality is improving, and new technologies are spreading. An Automated Fingerprint Identification System helps police at more than 80 agencies match fingerprints found at crime scenes to those in a national database. The system registers "hits" in more than 10 percent of cases. One area where quality remains suspect: the system of coroners and medical examiners. One reason is that only a few areas employ doctors trained to investigate unnatural deaths.

3. *Dangerous suspects commit crimes while awaiting trials on other charges.* Defendants have a legal right to be considered for release before trial, and nearly two thirds of those charged with serious

crimes—including one fourth of accused murderers—are allowed out on the street while awaiting trial. While most of them stay out of trouble, a disturbingly high 1 out of 3 either is rearrested, fails to appear in court on time or commits some infraction that results in a bail revocation. . . .

CRIMINAL TRIALS

4. *Prosecutors make bargains with too many criminals.* In 9 cases out of 10, no trial ever is held. The defendants accept plea bargains that let them plead guilty, usually to just a few of the charges. Critics argue that to move cases along, prosecutors too readily abandon charges that could bring tougher penalties. Although that does happen, just as common is overcharging—filing counts of dubious provability to pressure defendants.

A few places have moved to curb abuses. The most prominent example is Alaska, which banned plea bargaining in 1975. A study by the federal State Justice Institute found that the policy has improved the screening of cases and contributed to longer prison terms. However, researchers found that in some areas, bargaining over pleas has been replaced by bargaining over the charges filed.

VIOLENT CRIME IN AMERICA

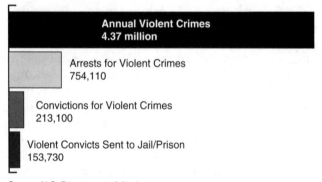

Annual Violent Crimes
4.37 million

Arrests for Violent Crimes
754,110

Convictions for Violent Crimes
213,100

Violent Convicts Sent to Jail/Prison
153,730

Source: U.S. Department of Justice

Ted Gest, *U.S. News & World Report*, October 9, 1995.

5. *Criminal cases take too long.* The interval between arrest and sentencing averages 274 days nationwide for murders and 172 days for violent crimes generally. The length of the few cases that go to trial is less of a problem. The National Center for State Courts reports that trials average about 11 hours, much shorter than the

time it took for single witnesses to testify in the Simpson extrav-
aganza. Murder trials typically last one to two weeks, depending
on the circumstances. California trials tend to take longer.

Still, "we can do a lot better" at expediting cases once they
reach court, says Barry Mahoney of the Denver-based Justice
Management Institute. Mahoney's group and others offer trial-
management training to judges, but probably fewer than 10
percent nationwide have taken it. A bigger problem: There aren't
enough judges to juggle all witnesses, defendants and lawyers
that come to court.

6. *The jury system is flawed.* It took 11 weeks to choose 12 jurors
and 12 alternates in the Simpson trial. Then, the jury was forced
to live in a hotel for nine months under guard, which frayed
nerves and cost taxpayers more than $2.5 million. The jury pro-
cess is so cumbersome, says Joseph DiGenova, former federal
prosecutor in Washington, D.C., that "procedures instituted a
century or two ago . . . are not adequate today."

Ideas abound to simplify jury service. Some reformers urge
curtailing the elaborate process of allowing prosecution and defense to eliminate potential jurors, often on the advice of expensive consultants who analyze candidates for expected biases.
Once the trial is underway, a few states, including Arizona, are
experimenting with permitting jurors to ask questions of witnesses. California prosecutors, noting that 14 percent of Los Angeles County trials end with a hung jury, are pressing the state
legislature to allow less-than-unanimous jury verdicts—which
Oregon and Louisiana already do.

7. *Trials are consumed more with tactics than truth.* Many believe that
defense lawyers search not for truth but for "preventing evidence of a defendant's guilt from reaching the jury," says James
Wootton of the Safe Streets Alliance, an anticrime group based
in Washington, D.C. Conservatives in Congress are trying to
blunt the "exclusionary rule," which prevents illegally obtained
evidence from being used in trials. They would allow such evidence if it was probably gathered in good faith. Others would
go further. Law Prof. Joseph Grano of Wayne State University advocates that defense lawyers be required to ask their clients
whether they committed the crime and to encourage the guilty
to accept responsibility.

But defense lawyers will resist basic changes. "It's been a long
time since I went to court looking for the truth," concedes Raymond Brown, a prominent Newark defense attorney. He says a
proper role of the defense is forcing prosecutors to prove guilt.

8. *Suspects get inadequate legal aid.* Simpson [has spent] millions on

a "dream team" defense. The reality for most criminal suspects is that they are fortunate to get much attention at all from over-worked public defenders or court-appointed attorneys. Most such advocates are competent: They achieve roughly the same results as high-priced attorneys. The problem is that there are too many cases and too little time. Experts say full-time defense lawyers should handle at most 150 felony cases each year. The actual number in many areas is much higher: Defenders in southwest Florida are assigned some 300 cases and up to 50 appeals a year.

Although a system of public defenders is in place, its resources are limited and declining. Congress, for example, is on the verge of eliminating federal funding for a network of centers that help defenders prepare cases of candidates for the death penalty. Critics say the centers help give attorneys ammunition to prolong cases unnecessarily; supporters respond that better sorting of the evidence can actually expedite trials and prevent needless appeals—not to mention helping ensure that innocent persons are not executed or put in prison for life.

Steve Benson. Reprinted by permission of United Feature Syndicate, Inc.

9. *Some criminals strike over and over.* A few criminals commit a disproportionate amount of violence, but identifying and incapacitating them has proved impossible. Limits on prison space and an inability to predict recidivists mean that nearly 6 of every 10 serious offenders are not sentenced to prison. More than 4 in 10

are arrested within three years for another serious crime. Of those who serve time, most are paroled before serving 40 percent of their time.

Several states are moving to abolish parole, and others are clamping down on early releases. Pennsylvania has slowed releases of violent offenders to a trickle. In South Carolina, retired naval officer Jim Grego founded Citizens Against Violent Crime 11 years ago when his daughter was seriously wounded in an assault by a twice-paroled felon. Now that the group has lobbied for tougher standards, the state paroles 25 to 30 percent of applicants compared with 75 percent a decade ago. Meanwhile, many states are beefing up habitual-offender laws, often by requiring life sentences for those who commit two or three violent offenses.

But get-tough measures can backfire. Some states that have eliminated parole have seen costs soar as prison populations explode. And in California, the "three strikes and you're out" law requiring life terms for third-time offenders is causing more defendants to demand trials, thus clogging the courts. "The real crisis in L.A. County is the impact of three strikes," says presiding trial Judge James Bascue.

10. The justice system is insensitive to the public, particularly crime victims. Except for their court testimony, victims traditionally have been shut out when penalties are assessed. This view is changing, albeit slowly. A growing crime-victims movement has succeeded in recognizing victim rights in most states, at least on paper. The challenge is giving those rights real meaning. Victims are campaigning for "restorative justice," a program to involve them more in the sentencing process. In many cases, that means requiring convicts to provide victims restitution for losses or encouraging assailants to face their victims.

Some courts, traditionally remote institutions, are acting to improve public relations. Connecticut indoctrinates its court employees in "total quality management," partly to help citizens seeking information about cases.

Many justice reforms require an infusion of tax money. "The public gets the justice system it pays for," says Donald Rebovich of the National District Attorneys Association. Other changes would necessitate fundamental rewriting of criminal law—something that has proved remarkably resistant to reform. Defense lawyers argue that the system generally works well, even if it results at times in a criminal's going free. So it's reasonable to expect that long after the Simpson case is over, the justice system will lurch along—and so will the public's frustration and outrage.

> "It is the mark of a higher
> civilization when a country finally
> chooses to eradicate . . . the damnable
> practice of killing for vengeance."

THE DEATH PENALTY SHOULD BE ELIMINATED

James McCloskey

In the following viewpoint, James McCloskey argues that not only is sentencing someone to death morally repugnant, but also that, in practical terms, the death penalty simply does not work. McCloskey charges that the death penalty is a dismal failure as a deterrent, primarily because those who commit crimes that merit the death penalty are often so irrational that even the prospect of the ultimate punishment does not deter them. Furthermore, he maintains, the death penalty is disproportionately expensive and has been applied in a discriminatory manner against minorities. McCloskey concludes that state-sanctioned killing degrades society and should be eradicated forever. McCloskey is the director of Centurion Ministries in Princeton, New Jersey.

As you read, consider the following questions:

1. In the author's opinion, why does Philadelphia's homicide rate suggest that the death penalty is an ineffective deterrent?
2. According to the author, how costly is the death penalty versus life imprisonment?
3. In McCloskey's view, which biblical passages support the abolition of the death penalty?

Reprinted from James McCloskey, "The Death Penalty: A Personal View," Criminal Justice Ethics, vol. 15, no. 2 (Winter/Spring 1996), pp. 2, 70–75, by permission of The Institute for Criminal Justice Ethics, 899 Tenth Ave., New York, NY 10019-1029.

What has it come to in this great nation of ours when the entire state and federal judiciary silently stood aside, as did the governor, and allowed Texas in 1995 to execute Jessie Jacobs, a man whose prosecutor even admitted was innocent of the shooting for which he was put to death? You think I exaggerate? Not so. You see, after Mr. Jacobs' conviction for the deadly shooting, the state of Texas conceded that it was Mr. Jacobs' sister, not Mr. Jacobs, who shot the woman. Although Mr. Jacobs forcibly took the female victim to his sister's house so that the two women could settle a dispute, Mr. Jacobs' own prosecutor later told the sister's jury that he now agreed that Mr. Jacobs had no idea the sister had a weapon or that she intended to use it and that Mr. Jacobs stood by in total surprise when she shot the woman to death.

For that, our esteemed machinery of justice puts a man to death? How hardboiled and desensitized a society have we become when our courts, with hardly a blink of the eye, behave in such a callous fashion? Jacobs' death must be laid at the feet of all those members of the judiciary—right up to the U.S. Supreme Court—for not stepping in and righting this wrong, thereby saving an innocent life. . . .

AN INEFFECTIVE DETERRENT

Most of those who are in favor of capital punishment concede that it is not a deterrent to murder. Philadelphia is rapidly gaining a reputation for being "the capital of capital punishment." Its current District Attorney, Lynne Abraham, is a zealot in pursuing the death penalty in cases when she can, probably more than any other prosecutor in the U.S., yet even she admits the death penalty is not a deterrent. Let us look at Philadelphia's homicide rate since Pennsylvania reinstituted the death penalty in 1978. From 1984 through 1990, when capital punishment had been in full swing for a number of years, the homicide rate dramatically and consistently increased as follows:

1984	263
1985	275
1986	346
1987	355
1988	402
1989	501
1990	525

In the same *Philadelphia Inquirer* article from which these figures are drawn, Manhattan District Attorney Morgenthau pointed out that in 1994 Manhattan reported 320 homicides, 21 percent fewer than Philadelphia. This is significant in that both counties are virtually the same in size of population, yet at that time New York did not have the death penalty while Pennsylvania did.

Besides that, murder is not a rational act done by rational people who carefully think through the consequences of their actions. Those who murder are usually either consumed by hate or anger or are in a warped emotional state. They are demented, pathological people who, at the time they kill, do so with utter disregard for human life. Many are either high on drugs or in desperate need for more drugs. Killers are by and large anti-social people who do not respond to such behavioral disincentives not to kill as the death penalty. Acceptance of normal societal values is alien to their individual natures. In my view, for us to think that we can influence or deter them from killing through capital punishment is in and of itself irrational thought and behavior.

DISPROPORTIONATELY EXPENSIVE

How about a more prosaic rationale for the abolition of the death penalty: money? District Attorney Morgenthau also made it clear in an opinion piece in the *New York Times* that since the death penalty does not deter murder, "the millions of dollars expended on it would be better spent on solutions—from prisons to drug treatment programs—that do." He went so far in another article as to declare that capital punishment hinders the fight against crime. Speaking of cost, it is important for us to understand how costly the death penalty is, vis-à-vis life imprisonment, and then make a judgement as to its economic value.

The most definitive study on this subject that I am aware of was done by two professors of public policy at Duke University and released in 1993. They studied the costs of every death penalty case (seventy-seven of them) in North Carolina in 1991 and 1992. This study concluded that the *extra cost* to the state of each execution actually carried out was $2.16 million. This means that it cost approximately $3 million to try, convict, sentence, litigate, house, and then finally execute a person, while it costs slightly over $1 million to secure and carry out a life imprisonment sentence.

According to my calculations based on this data, since there are now almost 3,000 people living on death row throughout the U.S., if each is executed, it will cost the U.S. $9 billion to accomplish this herculean task. Since life imprisonment for these 3,000 would cost $3 billion, the *extra cost* to the nation is $6 billion. In my view this is an absurd and complete waste of billions and billions of dollars which certainly could be used to combat crime in a far more effective and productive manner.

ARBITRARY APPLICATION

As of 1996, the death penalty exists in thirty-eight states. The local county district attorney has sole discretion on when to apply or seek its use. Thus, its application against the total number of homicides that occur in a county can be surprisingly sparing and selective, depending on the particular view of the local prosecutor. Consequently, its use as applied to very similar murders in different counties in the same state can be inconsistent and even contradictory.

In 1994 Pittsburgh's career prosecutor, Robert Colville, declared only 8 of 104 murders to be death penalty eligible while Philadelphia, the national leader, did the same in 159 out of 404 homicides. Mr. Colville told the *New York Times Magazine* that "I never had a lot of thought that the ultimate revenge was necessary. The death penalty can't cure everything." Dallas's District Attorney sought death only twice in 1994. Houston's long-term prosecutor, Johnny Holmes, sought death in only 10 percent of eligible 1994 homicides. Gil Garcetti asked for death in 18 of Los Angeles's 2,000 murders in 1994. He only got it in six cases. From 1990 to 1995, New Orleans juries issued death verdicts only twice. Chicago's Cook County obtained only seven death sentences in 1994.

With the advent of the death penalty in New York State in 1995, the Bronx District Attorney, Robert Johnson, has said that he will never seek the death penalty because of his "intense respect for the value and sanctity of human life." For all the hullabaloo over the death penalty across the nation, I think the above statistics, as they reveal how few murders in high-crime urban cities either qualify for the death penalty or involve the seeking of death, will shock most advocates of the death penalty. Given its relatively low use and its disproportionately high and exorbitant cost, my point is why even use it at all.

RACISM AND THE DEATH PENALTY

I agree with the 1972 U.S. Supreme Court which, in striking down the death penalty, characterized its application as "arbitrary" and "capricious" as well as "harsh and freakish. . . ." Its use is also racially biased against blacks. Historically, this has been the case, and in applying the death penalty to a rapidly expanding base of federal crimes, it still flagrantly discriminates against blacks.

From 1930 through 1980, 3,862 people were executed in the United States. Of these, 54 percent were black. Included in this number, 455 men were executed for rape, 90 percent of whom were black. During a great many of these years, blacks represented about 10 percent of the total population.

Mark Fiore. Reprinted by permission of the artist.

The situation somewhat improved from 1977, the year after the Supreme Court upheld the constitutionality of revised state capital punishment laws, through 1993. According to a U.S. Department of Justice 1994 report, 4,259 people entered death row during this period. Forty percent were black and 58 percent were white. Of the 226 people actually executed during these same 17 years, 39 percent were black and 53 percent were white. According to a 1994 Almanac, the black percentage of the total American population during these years was about 12 percent.

In 1991, for the first time in 50 years, a white man was executed for killing a black person. There are scores of examples in the reverse where a black person was executed for murdering a white. The implication of the way in which the death penalty has been administered in this nation is the not so subliminal message that a black person's life has less value attached to it than does the life of a white person. That is the way I read it, anyhow.

If you think that somehow we are becoming more sophisticated and therefore less discriminating in the way we administer the death penalty, look at what is happening in the federal system. There has not been a federal execution since the Rosenbergs in 1953. Since the expansion of the modern federal death penalty laws and procedures in 1988, the federal government has initiated approximately fifty death-case prosecutions. In order for a U.S. Attorney to do so, the procedures insist that he receive authorization by the U.S. Attorney General. Of the fifty capital prosecutions to date, 85 percent of the defendants are minorities. Here we go again!

KILLING FOR VENGEANCE

If the death penalty is so disproportionately costly and discriminatory against the poor and people of color, and if it is indisputable that it is not a deterrent and that innocent people get executed, then why do we do it and why is it so popular in the United States? It makes us "feel good" when we can unleash our anger and satisfy our deep seated need and desire for revenge. District Attorney Abraham of Philadelphia says it gives to citizenry a "feeling of control." District Attorney Morgenthau rebukes capital punishment by characterizing it as "violence in the name of vengeance." I believe that is why the public overwhelmingly sanctions it. Somehow it viscerally assuages not only our lust for vengeance but our outrage and helplessness at the unprecedented levels of bloodshed and violent crime throughout America.

Recently, a prominent resident of Princeton, whom I know only casually, stopped me on the street to declare that he believes in the death penalty because "even the Bible says an eye for an eye and a tooth for a tooth is how society should strike back at violence." That is true; the Old Testament does say this. However, as a Christian I believe in the ultimate authority of the words of Jesus Christ as presented in the Gospels of the New Testament.

In the Sermon on the Mount, as recorded in Matthew, Jesus says, "You have heard that it was said 'an eye for an eye and a tooth for a tooth.' But I say unto you. . . . [Further, that] if any one strikes you on one cheek turn the other to him . . . love your enemies." Also the Apostle Paul in his letter to the Romans urges them to "repay no one evil for evil" and to never avenge yourselves but leave it to the wrath of God for it is written, 'Vengeance is mine, I will repay,' says the Lord." Vengeance, as personified in capital punishment, in my view, is in direct opposition to the spirit of Christ.

Grounded as I am in these spiritual values, I find the death penalty to be morally repugnant. I do not believe the state should be in the killing business. It sends the wrong message. It tells society that if you at the bottom of society kill, we at the top of society will kill. As a result, the killing never stops, and peace will not come to the land. ✕

I would like to make one last point. Practically speaking, the death penalty simply does not work. Think of all the energy, anguish, and hard work expended by national and state legislatures, judges, prosecutors, police, juries, and attorneys, as well as the billions of dollars spent by the states and counties on behalf of capital punishment! Now consider this. According to a Department of Justice 1994 report, 42 percent of all death-row inmates between 1973 and 1993 were removed from death row primarily due to conviction/sentence reversals and commutations. This means that almost half of the convictions that resulted in the death penalty had serious constitutional flaws. Imagine the waste of money and resources in producing what turns out to be counterfeit death sentences in almost one out of every two instances.

As a result of the foregoing, I have thrown my lot in with former U.S. Supreme Court Justices Harry Blackmun and Lewis Powell, both of whom voted for the death penalty during their U.S. Supreme Court tenure. Just before retirement, in a 1994 dissent, Justice Blackmun wrote, "From this day forward, I no longer shall tinker with the machinery of death. . . . I feel morally and intellectually obligated to concede that the death penalty experiment has failed." Justice Powell told his biographer in 1994, "I have come to think that capital punishment should be abolished" because "it brings discredit to the whole system." Both of these men wrestled long and hard with capital punishment and came to see the complete futility of its usefulness.

All the nations of western continental Europe have abolished capital punishment, as have Canada (1976) and Great Britain (1971). In my view, it is the mark of a higher civilization when a country finally chooses to eradicate forever from its heart and soul the damnable practice of killing for vengeance. Eventually capital punishment will fall from its own weight. Future American generations will wonder in amazement how and why we continued capital punishment for as long as we did.

"If you choose to take another human life, you ought to be prepared to pay with your own."

THE DEATH PENALTY SHOULD NOT BE ELIMINATED

John Douglas

The former chief of the Investigative Support Unit of the FBI, John Douglas is a leading expert on criminal personality profiling. He is the author of numerous articles and books on criminology, including *Journey into Darkness*, from which the following viewpoint is excerpted. Douglas has studied firsthand some of the most dangerous criminals in the world, and he concludes that in many cases such remorseless crimes merit the ultimate sanction—the death penalty. To insist that a convicted murderer has the same right to live as the victim weakens the concept of right and wrong, according to Douglas. He maintains that the death penalty serves as an effective symbol of society's moral outrage at vicious criminal conduct.

As you read, consider the following questions:

1. According to Douglas, in what way is the death penalty a "specific deterrent"?
2. In the author's opinion, why is it inappropriate to keep heinous criminals alive for study purposes?
3. In Douglas's opinion, what type of criminals most deserve the death penalty?

Until we take seriously the most serious of crimes, we have no right to call ourselves civilized or enlightened. There are certain crimes that are simply too cruel, too sadistic, too hideous to be forgiven. . . .

But when I talk about punishment, aren't I really talking about vengeance—the biblical eye-for-an-eye concept? Maybe I am. Which brings up the next question: Does vengeance have a place in punishment?

Should punishment, as administered by the correctional system, be used as a therapeutic or cathartic tool for crime victims and their families? We all want them to have closure, but are they legally (as opposed to merely morally) entitled to it?

Jack and Trudy Collins [whose daughter Suzanne was raped, tortured, and killed by Sedley Alley in 1985] don't use the words "revenge" or "vengeance" to describe what it is they and others like them seek. "Though I don't disagree with the classic dictionary definition, 'to inflict deserved punishment for an injury,' for most people, they've now become emotionally loaded words with a connotation of personal malice, and their use ends up hurting the victim," Jack explains.

RETRIBUTION THROUGH PUNISHMENT

What they want, they say, is "retribution," which the Oxford English Dictionary defines as "recompense for, or requital of, evil done."

"It's a way of society balancing the scales," says Jack, "giving the victims and their families a feeling of satisfaction for what was done to them, to make them whole as far as possible or restore integrity—the quality or state of completeness—to both the people and the system. Nothing will ever bring Suzanne back to us. But even if this retribution doesn't bring complete closure, it shows us that society, the jury, and the entire criminal justice system care enough about us to see to it that our daughter's killer receives his appropriate punishment. It lets us know that they did right by us as far as they could."

It seems to me that for serious crimes, retribution through punishment is the only just and moral action that we, as a society, can take. This is not, however, a universal opinion.

As Jack Collins states, "Victims need to put the horror and trauma of the crime behind them as soon as possible and get on with their lives. Victims have a right to expect that defendants will be tried promptly so that, if convicted, their punishment can begin speedily. We've been trying to sensitize people to the fact that victims should not be considered outsiders in the criminal justice system. They have a stake; they should be in the forefront. We deserve and demand a place at the table."

When it comes to the next level of the criminal justice system, he says, "It seems to many observers of appeals courts, including ourselves, that too many of its judges consider the appellate function an academic and theoretical exercise that has more to do with intellectual sleight-of-hand and verbal dexterity than seeing that basic justice is done to victims and punishment meted out to wrongdoers. They appear to fancy the pose of being far above the fray, unaffected in any way by the blood, sweat, tears and violence which started the case's journey to their very chambers."

What the Collinses seek, of course, is the execution of their daughter's murderer in accord with the sentence handed down by his jury and judge.

Capital punishment is one of those issues like abortion. Not many of us are ever going to change anyone's opinion about it, one way or the other. If you are against the death penalty on moral grounds, I think a case can be made for putting away the worst of these monsters for life with no possibility they will ever be let out or paroled. But we know that there is no such thing. And frankly, in certain cases, I don't think it's enough.

As FBI special agent Steve Mardigian put it, "The tremendous devastation against victims warrants that we do something appropriately serious. In my view, we have no reason to keep people capable of inflicting this kind of horror alive."

SOCIETY'S MORAL STATEMENT

Some would argue that capital punishment is "legalized murder" and therefore an immoral act on the part of society. My personal feeling is that these offenders have made a choice to remove themselves from society and therefore it is a moral statement to say that society will not tolerate the perpetrator of this kind of horrible act in its midst.

Asserting that capital punishment is legalized murder does a tremendous injury, in my opinion, to the very concept of right and wrong, in that it trivializes the crucial distinction between the victim of the crime and its perpetrator—the innocent life and the one who chose for his own vile reasons to take that innocent life.

If you ask me if I'm personally prepared to throw the switch that would legally end the life on earth of [convicted murderers] Sedley Alley, Larry Gene Bell, Paul Bernardo, Lawrence Bittaker, or others of their ilk, my answer would be a resounding "Yes!" And for those who talk of forgiveness, I'll tell them I am sympathetic to the concept, but at the same time I do not feel I am authorized to forgive; it's not my place.

Had Sedley Alley merely (and I use this word with some trepidation) raped, beaten, and tortured Suzanne Collins, but left her alive and her mental faculties intact, then she, and only she, would have been in a position to forgive him if she so chose. And as far as I'm concerned, she remains the only one capable of forgiving him, but because of what actually did happen, she can only do so now after his jury-imposed sentence has been carried out.

That, I think, is what the Collinses mean by retribution rather than revenge.

DETERRENCE

Now, on the subject of deterrence, I admit that there can be little doubt that as presently administered in the United States, the death penalty is not a general deterrent to murder in many, if not most, situations. Common sense should tell us that if you're a young urban criminal making your living off the drug trade where there are huge amounts of money at stake and your business competition is out there trying to kill you every day, the dim prospect of a possible death sentence and execution somewhere at the end of a fifteen year procedural morass—that is, if you get caught, if you don't plea bargain, if you draw a tough judge and a tough jury, if you don't get reversed, if they don't change the law, et cetera, et cetera—isn't much of a deterrent, or a risk, for that matter, compared to the occupational hazards you face on the street every day of your working life. So let's be realistic about that aspect of the argument.

If the death penalty were applied more evenly and uniformly, and if the period of time from sentence to execution were reduced to a reasonable matter of months rather than a protracted period of years or even the decades that people like the Collinses have had to endure, then perhaps it would become more useful in dissuading would-be offenders in certain types of murders. But frankly, this theoretical speculation doesn't concern me all that much. Meted out fairly and consistently, perhaps the death penalty could become a general deterrent; I'm not certain and I wouldn't be optimistic about it.

But of one thing I am certain: it is, by God, a specific deterrent. No one who has been executed has ever taken another innocent life. And until such time as we really mean it as a society when we say "imprisonment for life," I, and the families of countless victims, would sleep better at night knowing there is no chance that the worst of these killers will ever again be able to prey on others. Even then, I personally believe that if you choose to take another human life, you ought to be prepared to pay with your own.

AN IMPERFECT JUSTICE SYSTEM

Our justice system is imperfect. Some monsters can be rehabilitated and go on to live useful and productive lives. Nathan Leopold, who partnered with Richard Loeb in the 1924 thrill killing of young Bobby Franks in Chicago, was paroled in 1958 and went on to finish out his years respectably and productively as a social worker and lab technician, volunteering for studies in malaria research. But you know something? I don't think that would be the case with a Lawrence Bittaker [convicted of the kidnap, rape, torture, and murder of teenage girls], and I'm not anxious to keep him around long enough to find out. Once you've done something this horrendous, you forfeit your claims to rehabilitation.

KILLERS FOR STUDY

Then there's the argument that rather than killing these guys, we should keep them alive "for study." I'm not sure what people mean by this; I don't think they know, themselves. I suppose they mean that if we study enough of them long enough, we'll figure out why they kill and what we can do to stop them.

Now as it happens, my colleagues at [the FBI headquarters at] Quantico, Virginia and I are among the few professionals who actually have studied these people. If anyone has a stake, therefore, in keeping them alive for intellectual reasons, it's us. And here's my response to that: If they're willing to talk to me at all, there is plenty of time during the protracted appeals process. If they're only willing to talk—as [serial killer] Ted Bundy ultimately was—as a bargaining chip for staying alive longer, then what they tell me is going to be tainted and self-serving anyway. When you tell me we should keep someone like Bundy alive to study, I say, "Fine, keep him alive six hours longer; that's all I need." I really don't think we're going to get much more beyond that.

I don't hate these people. Some of them, I even kind of liked. I happen to like [convicted murderer] Ed Kemper, for example. I got along with him well and we enjoyed good rapport. I respect his mind and his insight. Had he been given the death penalty, I would have been personally sorry and sad to see him executed. But I certainly wouldn't have been willing to argue the point with the families of any of his victims, because I know what they've gone through and continue to go through. Compared to their feelings, mine are irrelevant.

But no responsible discussion of the death penalty can fail to include reflection on the fact that our legal system is imperfect and there is always the chance that the wrong man will be convicted. Inevitably, in any consideration of capital punishment, we must confront the example of David Vasquez [who was convicted of murder and later found innocent]. . . .

Reprinted by permission of Chuck Asay and Creators Syndicate.

The fact that this was a rare, odd type of case in which the defendant actually confessed, not once, but three times, should not give us too much comfort or reassurance. At the same time, I don't think this is a valid argument for scrapping the death penalty altogether.

A MOUNTAIN OF EVIDENCE

What I think it is a valid argument for is the insistence on an overwhelming amount and degree of proof. And while some might argue that you can never be absolutely sure, I think in the kinds of cases I'm talking about, you can be sure enough that innocent people like Vasquez will not go wrongly to their deaths.

The types of offenders I most want to see face the ultimate

penalty are the repeat, predatory, sexually motivated killers. By the time we catch them there is generally a mountain of solid, behaviorally consistent, forensic evidence against them. As with [serial killer] Cleophus Prince, if he did one of the murders, he did all of them. If there isn't a sufficiently formidable mountain of evidence, then don't execute. But if there is, as there was against Bell, as there is against Alley and Bernardo and Bittaker and so many others, then do what needs to be done.

PERIODICAL BIBLIOGRAPHY

The following articles have been selected to supplement the
diverse views presented in this chapter. Addresses are provided
for periodicals not indexed in the *Readers' Guide to Periodical Literature*, the *Alternative Press Index*, the *Social Sciences Index*, or the *Index to
Legal Periodicals and Books*.

Stephen Adler	"Juries on Trial," *American Legion*, June 1995. Available from 5561 W. 74th St., Indianapolis, IN 46268.
Robert L. Carter	"The Criminal Justice System Is Infected with Racism," *Vital Speeches of the Day*, March 1, 1996.
CQ Researcher	"The Jury System," November 10, 1995. Available from 1414 22nd St. NW, Washington, DC 20037.
George P. Fletcher	"Convicting the Victim," *New York Times*, February 7, 1994.
Ken Hamblin	"The Courts Are Colorblind," *Conservative Chronicle*, January 1, 1997. Available from PO Box 29, Hampton, IA 50441.
Jeff Herman	"Justice Gone Awry? How to Get the U.S. Jury System Back on Track," *Vital Speeches of the Day*, December 1, 1996.
Patrick A. Langan	"No Racism in the Justice System," *Public Interest*, Fall 1994.
Peter Linebaugh	"Gruesome Gertie at the Buckle of the Bible Belt," *New Left Review*, January/February 1995.
Marc Mauer and Tracy Huling	"Young Black Americans and the Criminal Justice System: Five Years Later," *Sentencing Project*, October 1995. Available from 918 F. St. NW, Suite 501, Washington, DC 20004.
George E. Pataki	"The Death Penalty Brings Justice," *Corrections Today*, August 1996. Available from the American Correctional Assoc., Inc., 4380 Forbes Blvd., Lanham, MD 20706-4322.
Victor Perlo	"Criminalization of African Americans," *Political Affairs*, February 1995.
Ricardo Ramirez	"Prison Reform and the Ideals of Justice," *Origins*, March 2, 1995. Available from the Catholic News Service, 3211 4th St. NE, Washington, DC 20017-1100.
Richard Stratton	"The End of Rehabilitation," *Prison Life*, October 1996. Available from PO Box 537, Stone Ridge, NY 12484.

DO THE RIGHTS OF THE ACCUSED UNDERMINE THE CRIMINAL JUSTICE SYSTEM?

CHAPTER PREFACE

Historically, the U.S. Supreme Court has struggled to keep a balance between criminals' rights and the need to apprehend and punish criminals. One of the most publicized—and criticized—criminal procedure cases was the 1966 landmark *Miranda vs. Arizona*. In that case, Ernesto Miranda was identified in a police lineup for the kidnapping and rape of an eighteen-year-old woman. At the time, custodial questioning of lawfully arrested suspects carried no special requirement obliging police to inform suspects of their rights. When police questioned Miranda, he signed a written confession that resulted in his conviction and lengthy prison sentence. While in prison, he complained that he had not been informed of his rights guaranteed under the Fifth Amendment, which provides that no person may be compelled to be a witness against himself. In a ruling that shocked the nation, Miranda's conviction was overturned. From that point on, police must warn a suspect in custody that he has the right to remain silent, that any statements he makes might be used against him, and that he has the right to counsel.

According to its detractors, the *Miranda* rule hinders law enforcement. Police officers and others contend that *Miranda* encourages a suspect to withhold valuable information and also provides a legal loophole that may allow a guilty criminal to go free. Dissenting Supreme Court justice Byron R. White's harsh indictment of *Miranda* was widely quoted after the ruling: "In some unknown number of cases, the court's rule will return a killer, rapist or other criminal to the streets and to the environment which produced him, to repeat his crime whenever it pleases him." Today, many believe that White's predictions have been fulfilled. Calling for tougher crime laws, harsher punishments, and fewer constraints on police, these critics maintain that *Miranda* should be abolished.

Others insist that *Miranda* has not impeded the flow of confessions or resulted in the freeing of droves of guilty criminals. Most importantly, they charge, the *Miranda* warning remains a bulwark against police coercion, an aid to the poor and uneducated who may be at a disadvantage in the criminal justice system. "It was no accident that Miranda was an unlearned man," noted attorney John Frank, who represented Ernesto Miranda. "*Miranda* is the Constitution's insurance for the uneducated."

Although most Americans agree that the accused should have rights within the criminal justice system, the extent of these rights is debated. This issue is seminal to all of the articles presented in the following chapter.

"Every time we protect the rights of a stranger, we reaffirm the sanctity and safety of our own constitutional rights."

THE RIGHTS OF THE ACCUSED MUST BE ZEALOUSLY PROTECTED

Sol Wachtler

According to Sol Wachtler, fear of crime is rampant, fueling a public outcry for judicial crackdown on criminals, including diminishing legal protections for the accused. Wachtler argues in the following viewpoint that these admonitions are misguided and that lessening the rights of the accused would put the criminal justice system in jeopardy. By preserving the safeguards in the Bill of Rights, Wachtler maintains, the protection of the law will be available—and will be applied evenly—to all citizens. Wachtler has had the unusual experience of viewing the criminal justice system from both sides of the bench; in addition to serving as a chief judge of the New York State Court of Appeals, Wachtler was recently prosecuted and convicted of aggravated harassment, completing a prison sentence for the crime.

As you read, consider the following questions:

1. According to Wachtler, how have politicians fueled society's appetite for judicial reform?
2. In Wachtler's opinion, why should the power of prosecutors be kept in check?
3. According to Charles Silberman, as quoted by the author, how effective are criminal courts?

Reprinted from Sol Wachtler, "Crime and Punishment," New Yorker, July 15, 1996, by permission of the author.

"**I**s a society redeemed if it provides massive safeguards for accused persons . . . and yet fails to provide elementary protection for its law-abiding citizens?" So asked Chief Justice Warren Burger, of the United States Supreme Court, in a 1981 address to the American Bar Association. The question is one that is repeated today—not quite so artfully phrased—by public-office holders and seekers from both political parties. Indeed, there is an increasing consensus among Americans that those "massive safeguards" have grown beyond all reason, elevating the rights of criminals above those of their victims. "Public opinion's always in advance of the law," John Galsworthy said. If he was right, we can look forward to changes in the law which will make Chief Justice Burger's recommendations sound like an American Civil Liberties Union manifesto.

It's little wonder that the typical American seems convinced that the courts are to blame for the crime in the streets. In count-less movies and TV shows, murderous villains are released "on a technicality." Somebody failed to read them their rights, or a crucial piece of evidence was suppressed on procedural grounds, or a lenient judge has bought their sob story and is letting them off with a slap on the wrist. And this picture of the courts as a place where the guilty hold sway is reinforced every day by poli-ticians deploring soft-hearted and soft-headed judges who, we are told, care more about criminals than about their victims.

On the campaign trail in 1996, former presidential candidate Bob Dole and Clinton alike sometimes appeared to be running against the judicial system: when a federal judge made a contro-versial ruling that excluded drug evidence, the two candidates, in chorus, called for his resignation or removal from the bench. Several bills are pending in Congress which would deprive judges of certain decision-making powers, particularly with re-spect to the operation of the exclusionary rule in federal courts. Both former candidates . . . endorsed a "victims' rights" amend-ment to the Constitution. Meanwhile, a call for rigid "manda-tory sentencing" for violent crimes . . . assumed a place along-side calls for the restoration of the death penalty as a major plank in most political-campaign platforms.

PRESERVING CONSTITUTIONAL PROTECTIONS

Advocates of such "reforms" maintain that they are necessary to insure that the guilty are punished, their victims vindicated. The arguments are compelling, but are they right? As Chief Judge of the New York State Court of Appeals, I had the task of reviewing records of criminal trials where defendants alleged that they had been wronged by the courts; more often than not, I voted to uphold the conviction. Unlike my judicial colleagues, however, I have had the experience of being prosecuted and convicted, and I recently completed a prison sentence (for the crime of aggravated harassment). Defendants appealing their convictions were no longer simply names on a court docket; they were in the next cell. The experience has only confirmed my view of the criminal-justice system—that the system must work to punish the guilty without lessening the constitutional protections accorded all citizens. And it's still clear to me that the two objectives aren't genuinely in conflict. . . .

If civil liberties have never been inconsistent with the aggressive and efficient prosecution of crime, neither can the rights of suspects be dismissed as some aberration of a left-leaning Warren Court. The Bill of Rights came into being because our founders had experienced the power of the crown in trammelling liberty. Four of the amendments in the Bill of Rights were designed to protect the prisoner in the dock—to make certain that the freedom granted the citizens of this new nation was not eclipsed by prosecutorial abuse.

INVITING ABUSE

Yet lately we have been enacting laws that virtually invite this abuse, by empowering the prosecutor to control the criminal-justice process from beginning (the grand jury) to end (sentencing under the mandated guidelines). Judge Harold Rothwax is typical of those who believe that the prosecutor must be given the upper hand over defense counsel. "In a court of law, only the prosecution is assigned the task of seeking the truth," he claims. Yet the fact is that defense attorneys, unlike prosecutors, have no inherent power over the system. And when the powers of prosecutors are expanded so are the possibilities of abuse. . . .

A society that lives in fear of crime behind triple-locked doors is an easy target for the political rhetoricians who suggest that diminishing constitutional protections will lead to safer streets. I suspect that ever since Miranda [establishing a universal standard that required all persons in police custody to be read their rights before being questioned] and the exclusionary rule became effective the public has believed that constitutional safeguards are freeing guilty criminals in droves. Nobody has told the public that confessions seem to be given as freely and readily now as they were before the Miranda decision, or that convictions, too, are still being obtained as they should be, with between ninety and ninety-five per cent of them guilty pleas. As

Charles Silberman concluded in his book *Criminal Violence, Criminal Justice* (1978), "criminal courts generally do an effective job of separating the innocent from the guilty, most of those who should be convicted are convicted, and most of those who should be punished are punished." Worse still, the demagogic attacks on judges for being "soft on crime" pay scant heed to the tradition of an independent judiciary. A restless public is told that if judges were tougher on crime there would be less crime. But the fact is that the courts don't cause crime and the judges can't prevent crime. They are, as Judge David Bazelon once said, like "janitors, tidying up the human and social wreckage." Similarly, it is a great mistake to regard the courts and the judges as quiet implementers or expediters of the prosecutor's office or of the position taken by the government. They are supposed to be the guardians of justice in our society in accordance with the law. If our judicial system has a single outstanding feature, it is its attempt to apply the law fairly and with an even hand—free from the passions of the moment and free from the passions of the crowd. Courts are not branch offices of the executive or of the legislature; they are a separate branch of the government.

We do not provide criminal defendants with constitutional

PRESUMPTION OF GUILT

If you don't want to spend time in jail, don't commit a crime. This statement sounds simple enough and widely is accepted as the truth, but in reality it is far from accurate; innocence doesn't protect someone automatically from incarceration, or even from execution. . . .

The public wants wrongdoers to be punished and friends, families, and neighbors to be protected. With some exceptions, the people who make up the legal system want the same things, but their zeal to convict the guilty sometimes imprisons the innocent.

The average citizen believes that, for someone to be arrested and, especially, brought to trial, he or she must have done something wrong. This simply is not true. A single false accusation is enough to get somebody arrested, and potentially put behind bars. . . .

Those fighting to preserve protections for the accused are charged with being soft on crime because it is impossible to protect the innocent without also protecting the guilty. By and large, the public just doesn't believe that innocent people can be and are arrested, jailed, convicted, and sometimes even sentenced to death.

Anne Martinez, *USA Today*, May 1995.

---

protections for their benefit alone. We do it for ourselves as well. Every time we protect the rights of a stranger, we reaffirm the sanctity and safety of our own constitutional rights. We also affirm that if the day comes when we, or those dear to us, need the protection of the law the protection will be there. That's something I believed during my years on the bench, and something I really learned once I left it.

"A criminal justice system that
contorts itself to the extreme in a
purported effort 'to protect the
accused'... is a system which has
lost its sight and soul."

ZEALOUS PROTECTION OF THE RIGHTS OF THE ACCUSED WEAKENS THE CRIMINAL JUSTICE SYSTEM

Daniel Lungren

Daniel Lungren is California's attorney general. In the following
viewpoint, Lungren derides a justice system that places a high
priority on the rights of criminals. He contends that the primary
goal of the criminal justice system is to protect the innocent from
perpetrators of crime, a goal that becomes muddled when offenders assume the position of victim. This happens, Lungren asserts, when lawyers for the accused focus on police misconduct,
for example, rather than the guilt or innocence of the perpetrator.
Society can restore justice and credibility to a faltering system,
Lungren urges, by being an advocate for the crime victim.

As you read, consider the following questions:

1. Why does Lungren believe that the case of Robert Alton
   Harris is a good example of justice gone awry?
2. According to Lungren, from what perspectives can we view
   the criminal justice system?
3. In the author's opinion, why are prisoner lawsuits
   inappropriate?

Reprinted from Daniel E. Lungren, "Victims and the Exclusionary Rule," *Harvard Journal of Law and Public Policy*, vol. 19 (Spring 1996), pp. 695–701, by permission of the publisher.

I was at San Quentin on the night of April 20–21, 1992, for the execution of Robert Alton Harris—the first execution in California in twenty-five years. As the chief law enforcement officer of the State of California, I am responsible for notifying the warden when all legal checks have been made and no impediments remain for a scheduled execution. Enforcing a death-penalty sentence is not a fun thing to do, but it must be done. That night we made history because we went up four times to the United States Supreme Court in six hours, confronting four different stays offered by a total of eleven different federal judges.

We had anticipated every claim to be made against the right of the State to carry out that execution by completing anticipatory briefs. We filed them with the United States Supreme Court, the Court of Appeals for the Ninth Circuit, the California Supreme Court, and the relevant district court. We logged them (we did not file them, because there was nothing for us to respond to at the time); then, as more than one thousand documents flowed in over the last week (and this was over an Easter weekend), we would call up the clerk of the relevant court and tell him to activate the appropriate brief.

On the occasion of the second stay, I sought out the mother of one of the fifteen-year-old boys who had been brutally murdered more than thirteen years before by Harris. I explained our strategy in responding to the second stay order and that we expected to be successful. She took a deep breath and said to me, "Oh, I get it: it's like a chess game." I have dedicated my professional life to the writing and enforcement of the law, and that remark hit me like a cold blast of wind. My only reply was, "It should not be a game at all, it should be about justice." That event summarizes where we are in the criminal justice system on the whole question of victimology.

ELUSIVE JUSTICE

Are we, in fact, involved in the pursuit of justice? Or are we sidetracked with certain types of gamesmanship? In Los Angeles today, and throughout California, there are many people who truly believe that the police routinely victimize citizens accused of crime—by planting evidence, breaking into homes or offices, using unnecessary force, or actively discriminating on the basis of race or ethnicity. The Rodney King experience and the Mark Fuhrman tapes come swiftly to the minds of the pundits who explore the question of police misconduct in our criminal justice system. Even as long ago as 1971, William Ryan's book Blaming the Victim portrayed the urban rioters of the late 1960s as oppressed and impatient idealists who merely engaged in a little property damage and portrayed the police and other repressive forces of law and order as truly violent to a homicidal degree.

Although no one condones police misconduct (my office acts in many ways to root it out throughout the State), we ought to consider the rest of society that regularly is victimized. The perpetrators' lawyers seek every opportunity to make the issue at trial become police conduct, not the guilt or innocence of the accused. Over the past thirty years, the criminal defense bar and the courts have shaped our criminal procedure and courtroom practice, in the face of congressional legislative acquiescence and abdication, in such a way that criminal defendants can scapegoat the police and go free, as Judge Cardozo put it, "because the constable has blundered."

© Dan Foote/*Dallas Times Herald*. Reprinted by permission of Texas International News Features.

We have apparently forgotten Adam Smith's admonition that mercy to the guilty is cruelty to the innocent. In this regard, we must remind ourselves that we can adopt many different perspectives from which to view the criminal justice system. For example, we can choose the viewpoint of the accused, the prosecutor, the judge, the defense attorney, or the police investigator. Remarkable clarity is achieved when we assume the perspective of the crime victim. After all, the only reason for a criminal justice system is to protect the law-abiding from law-breaking predators.

A criminal justice system that contorts itself to the extreme in a purported effort "to protect the accused," with the result that the innocent victim is denied justice (which includes retribution), is a system which has lost its sight and soul and forfeited its right to be called "just" or justice. Extending the definition of victim so broadly that it includes perpetrators devalues the plight of those who truly are victimized. I urge you not to forget the true victims of crime: those who have been violently assaulted by others, and the families of victims. . . .

THE EXCLUSIONARY RULE

The exclusionary rule is used to ban most courtroom use of unlawfully seized evidence. The Supreme Court originally adopted the exclusionary rule for the federal criminal prosecutions in 1914, in *Weeks v. United States*. In 1961, the Court extended it to the States in *Mapp v. Ohio*. I believe it is clear, however, that the rule is not constitutionally compelled. As the Court argued in *United States v. Leon*, the rule is strictly "a judicially created remedy designed to safeguard Fourth Amendment rights generally through its deterrent effect, rather than a personal constitutional right of the party aggrieved." As the *Leon* Court explained, the Fourth Amendment contains no provision expressly precluding the use of evidence obtained in violation of its commands. . . .

Certainly the Framers of the Constitution did not contemplate, nor did the common law of 1789 mandate, the suppression of unlawfully obtained evidence. Undoubtedly such evidence, which is in any case highly reliable evidence, was admissible as to the guilt or innocence of the accused.

Thus as a society, we need now to examine whether the rule serves any of its purported purposes, and I suggest we examine the rule from the perspective of the victim of the crime that was committed. Some, such as Judge Henry Friendly, have suggested that the exclusionary rule supplies a benefit "wholly disproportionate to the wrong suffered" by the guilty because even a minor error by the police can lead to the suppression of evidence and the inability to prosecute a clearly guilty offender. . . .

PROTECT THE INNOCENT

The criminal justice system was set up to protect the innocent from the predators. If, in our specific approach to protecting the accused, we go so far that the innocent are put at risk, have we undermined the credibility of the system itself? . . .

The impact of the judicially oriented metamorphosis from crime perpetrator to society's victim is probably felt nowhere greater than in federal habeas corpus death penalty cases. It is extremely difficult to explain to individuals thirteen and fifteen years after a crime has taken place, and a judgment of guilt and a sentence of death has been rendered, why there is no finality. Yet it is not the accused but the convicted murderer who assumes the position of victim in most habeas cases.

Prisoner lawsuits also assume that those who are imprisoned are the victims as opposed to the perpetrators. Some insist that it is the prison's mission to punish prisoners and hence to maintain and reinforce an imbalance of power, and that the judiciary is properly concerned with providing a redress to that imbalance of power. This is nonsense.

There ought to be an imbalance of power between those who have been convicted of crimes and those who are in charge of the system. To suggest that the federal courts are there to redress that imbalance is victimology run amuck. It is just another example of how we have to address this problem directly, not to get rid of our constitutional protections, but to right our system so that it is not perceived as a system which revictimizes the true victims of crime.

"The single most damaging legacy of the Supreme Court's criminal-justice revolution of the 1960s [is] the Miranda rule."

THE MIRANDA RULE UNDERMINES THE CRIMINAL JUSTICE SYSTEM

Paul Cassell and Stephen J. Markman

"You have the right to remain silent. . . ." Few words are as thoroughly embedded in the public consciousness as the police officer's incantation to a suspect in custody. Created by the Warren Court in 1966, the Miranda rule grants suspects the right to remain silent and to have an attorney present during questioning, allegedly serving as a bulwark against police abuse of power. Yet Paul Cassell and Stephen J. Markman argue in the following viewpoint that the Miranda rule has had a devastating effect on the criminal justice system. Cassell and Markman contend that the Miranda rule dangerously compromises law enforcement efforts because it impedes police from obtaining valuable information— namely blocking confessions—during police interrogations. The result, they maintain, is that guilty criminals who might otherwise be convicted are turned loose to revictimize society. Paul Cassell is a professor at the University of Utah College of Law. Stephen J. Markman is a judge of the Michigan Court of Appeals.

As you read, consider the following questions:

1. In the authors' view, how did the Fifth Amendment prohibit self-incrimination before Miranda?
2. In the authors' opinion, why are confessions desirable?
3. According to Cassell and Markman, how did the Miranda decision affect confession rates?

Reprinted, with permission, from Paul Cassell and Stephen J. Markman, "Miranda's Hidden Costs," National Review, December 25, 1995; ©1995 by National Review, Inc., 215 Lexington Ave., New York, NY 10016.

Curiously absent from the debate within Congress about how to combat historically unprecedented levels of violent crime in the United States has been any serious discussion of the single most damaging legacy of the Supreme Court's criminal-justice revolution of the 1960s: the Miranda rule. While intensive debate has focused upon other aspects of the Court's revolution—for example, the exclusionary rule and novel forms of habeas-corpus review—Miranda today seems little more than an anachronistic remnant of the era of "Impeach Earl Warren" billboards.

One possible explanation for this development is that the impact of Miranda, while extraordinarily detrimental to the criminal-justice system, is largely a hidden one, while the costs of such innovations as the exclusionary rule and habeas corpus are highly visible, in the form of kilos of cocaine being removed from the courtroom and repetitive criminal appeals inundating the justice system. Indeed, the costs of Miranda are so obscured that even many law-enforcement officers are only vaguely aware of them. Estimating the costs of Miranda requires that we engage in the difficult exercise of comparing the present reality with the reality which might exist "but for" the rule.

For tens of millions of Americans, the Miranda warnings have been learned from countless televised police dramas in which arrested suspects have been apprised by conscientious police officers that "You have the right to remain silent; what you say may be used against you; you have a right to an attorney; and you have a right to a free attorney if you cannot afford one." Few of those who have long since memorized these innocuous words have paused to consider how they have eroded the ability of the criminal-justice system to carry out its responsibilities.

MIRANDA V. ARIZONA

In its 1966 decision in Miranda v. Arizona, the Supreme Court by a 5 to 4 vote determined that the Fifth Amendment's prohibition against a person's being "compelled in any criminal case to be a witness against himself" required what have become known as the Miranda warnings whenever a witness in custody is subject to questioning by the police. The decision also required that police obtain a "waiver of rights" from a suspect—that is, an affirmative agreement from the suspect that he would like to talk to police. Also, if at any time the suspect indicated a wish to stop talking or to see a lawyer, police had to stop questioning immediately. Failure to deliver the warnings, obtain the waiver, or cut off questioning when requested automatically bars the use at trial of statements obtained from the suspect.

Underlying *Miranda* was a deep suspicion on the part of the Court majority about any custodial interrogation of criminal suspects. For the 175 years preceding *Miranda*, it had never been thought that the police were violating a suspect's constitutional rights merely by questioning him in the absence of an attorney. No, we are not referring to a police officer's beating the hapless suspect with a rubber hose or policemen working in shifts to keep the suspect from sleep until he finally confesses to a crime. Such tactics were condemned uniformly well before *Miranda*. To satisfy the requirements of the Fifth Amendment, a confession needed to be voluntary, and circumstances which called that voluntariness into doubt served to undermine the admissibility of a confession. Confessions occur for any number of reasons, including the simple desire to cleanse one's soul and the more complicated desire to explain extenuating circumstances. Under the voluntariness standard, police were not precluded from asking the suspect what knowledge he possessed about the dead body they had discovered buried in his backyard.

AMENDING THE CONSTITUTION

This old understanding of the Fifth Amendment's prohibition against coerced self-incrimination was sharply transformed by *Miranda*. The Court acknowledged that "it might not find the defendant's statements to have been involuntary in traditional terms." In other words, the *Miranda* decision was amending the Constitution. In place of the previous understanding, the Court effectively provided a criminal suspect with a right not to be questioned. If he was questioned prior to the warnings, any statements would be suppressed; if he was questioned after the warnings and after he had requested an attorney, any statements that were made prior to the attorney's arrival again would be suppressed. After the attorney's arrival, it was certain that there would be no statements at all.

In dissent, Justice Byron White observed, "In some unknown number of cases the Court's rule will return a killer, a rapist, or other criminal to the streets and to the environment which produced him to repeat his crime whenever it pleases him. As a consequence there will not be a gain, but a loss, in human dignity." Justice White was prescient, although it can hardly be imagined that the majority of Justices in *Miranda* disagreed with his assessment. Such a result was logically certain under *Miranda*.

The insidiousness of *Miranda* is that, by and large, the violent predators placed back on the streets are not suspects to whom police have failed to give proper warnings. After nearly three decades, the police not surprisingly have learned *Miranda* by rote and only rarely fail to administer its warnings or follow its waiver and questioning-cutoff rules. Relatively few criminal cases involve the suppression of evidence obtained by police after a failure to comply with *Miranda*. This is what many observers, including some law-enforcement officers themselves, mean when they contend that the system has "learned to live" with *Miranda*.

BLOCKING VALUABLE EVIDENCE

No, the enormous cost of *Miranda* is entailed not in the lapses of the system but in its successes. It is when the warnings are properly administered and waiver rules are followed that it wreaks its greatest harm. For what it has done is to substantially dry up access to a hugely important category of criminal evidence—confession evidence. It is almost as if the Supreme Court had told law-enforcement officials that, henceforth, they were no longer going to be able to use fingerprint evidence. No one would doubt that in "some unknown number of cases" individuals who would otherwise have been correctly identified as criminals would avoid prosecution.

Principally, *Miranda* has eroded the supply of information available to law enforcement by introducing the criminal's defense attorney to the process at the earliest possible stage. This is done, in a sense, by the suspect asserting his *Miranda* right to have an attorney present at questioning even before formal charges have been filed. The effect of this is to preclude entirely the questioning of many suspects because police recognize that such questioning would be pointless. By effectively insulating the suspect who invokes his rights or asks for a lawyer from any questioning, no matter how restrained or reasonable, *Miranda* has assured that far fewer confessions will be induced by questioning. For the *Miranda* majority, this was cause for celebration, not concern. But this is an odd—not to say dangerous—view of the world. As an earlier Supreme Court said, "the Constitution is not at all offended when a guilty man stubs his toe. On the contrary, it is decent to hope that he will." The principal legacy of *Miranda* is the creation of an environment in which everything possible has been done to avoid such self-inflicted injuries. Given the relatively modest intellectual faculties of many violent criminals, the incidence of such injuries had always been significant.

If the criminal suspect incriminates himself through police methods that do not involve compulsion, that is a good thing. It is a good thing because it results in accurate fact-finding by the criminal-justice system; it avoids the possibility that an innocent person might be charged with a crime he did not commit; and it promotes public confidence that the police have caught the right person. In other words, it is a good thing because it promotes justice through procedures which most Americans would view as fair.

The most compelling evidence of the desirability of confessions, and of the extent to which Justice White's warnings have been borne out, comes from the before-and-after studies done in the immediate wake of the decision in 1966. One leading study, done in Philadelphia, reported that, before Miranda, an estimated 45 per cent of all criminal suspects made confessions to police officers; following Miranda, that figure dropped to approximately 20 per cent. Another study, done in New York City, found that confession rates fell from 49 per cent to 15 per cent. In Pittsburgh, the confession rate among suspected robbers and murderers fell from 60 per cent to 30 per cent. Adverse effects on confessions were also reported in Chicago, Kansas City, Brooklyn, and New Orleans. The best-estimate consensus among all the studies done on the impact of Miranda is that a lost confession occurs in approximately one of every six, or 16 per cent, of all criminal cases in the United States.

DECLINES IN CONFESSION RATES

The other leading methodology for such calculations, albeit less exact, is to compare the American confession rate after Miranda with confession rates in countries that follow different approaches to regulating police interrogations. Such comparisons fully confirm the conclusions of the before-and-after studies. Since Miranda, American police appear to obtain confessions in perhaps 40 per cent of all cases. In other countries, police are far more successful. In Great Britain in the 1970s and early 1980s, police, following the "Judges' Rules," gave only a very limited advice of rights. Confession rates were estimated to be 61 to 85 per cent, well above reported American rates. In Canada, confession rates also appear to be substantially higher than in the post-Miranda United States.

Such declines in confession rates as have occurred in the United States since Miranda are extraordinarily harmful to the interests of effective law enforcement. Confession evidence, because it comes from the perpetrator himself, is compelling; but it doesn't stand alone—it is virtually always subject to corroboration by physical or other evidence. According to the available studies, in about one-quarter (24 per cent) of all criminal cases, confessions or other self-incriminating statements by a suspect are indispensable to a criminal conviction; in many more cases, perhaps an equal number, it can be surmised that they make some difference in terms of the severity of the offense for which a defendant is convicted.

OVERRULING MIRANDA

I call *Miranda* the triumph of formalism. In my judgment, *Miranda* should be repudiated. It's bad constitutional law. It's ill-conceived policy. And most grievous, it has created a jurisprudence of formalism. . . .

These are the reasons *Miranda* should be overruled:

- *Miranda* is not a wise or necessary decision—nor a harmless one.

- *Miranda* has sent our jurisprudence on a hazardous detour by introducing novel conceptions of the proper relationship between a criminal suspect and a law enforcement officer.

- *Miranda* has accentuated just those features in our system that manifest the *least* regard for truth-seeking: the view that the process is a game of chance in which the defendant should always have some prospect of victory.

- *Miranda* was decided at a time when effective alternatives for restraining unlawful police conduct were ripe for implementation but were subsequently never pursued.

- The meaning of *Miranda* has not become reasonably clear, as its advocates contend. Rather, technical issues continue to abound about its meaning and scope.

Harold J. Rothwax, *Guilty: The Collapse of Criminal Justice*, 1996.

A rough calculation, then, can be made as to the real-world cost of the *Miranda* rules. Multiplying the estimated 16-point reduction in the confession rate after *Miranda* by the estimated 24 per cent of cases in which a confession was necessary for conviction produces a figure of 4 per cent of all criminal cases that will be "lost" or never successfully prosecuted because of the rules. That figure may not sound very high, but the cost in absolute numbers of criminal cases is staggering. For FBI-index crimes, each year *Miranda* results in approximately 28,000 "lost" cases for violent crimes (murder, rape, aggravated assault, and robbery) and 79,000 "lost" cases for serious property crimes (burglary, larceny, and car theft). The bare numbers do not begin to convey the human costs in murders that go unpunished, rapists who remain at large, and treasured heirlooms that are never recovered.

Additionally, the leverage of prosecutors would be reduced in a roughly equal number of cases, resulting in plea bargains more favorable to the defendant and less favorable to the public. Compare these figures with the likely gains expected from other crime-control measures, such as midnight basketball leagues or even long-overdue habeas corpus reform. It seems improbable that any other single needed change in the criminal-justice system would yield anywhere near the number of successful prosecutions that would result from repealing *Miranda*.

Further, all these figures must be weighed in the light of other figures from the Bureau of Justice Statistics indicating that roughly two-thirds of all violent crime in the United States is committed by repeat offenders. *Miranda* does not merely defeat justice in the immediate case, but prematurely returns to the streets individuals in this high-risk category. . . .

ALTERNATIVES TO MIRANDA

Ironically, there are better means of enforcing the very protections toward which *Miranda* is directed. However, as is the case generally with the exercise of uniform national policies, *Miranda* petrified efforts by the states, which were widespread in the 1960s, to experiment with their custodial interrogation procedures and search for alternatives that might better protect not only society's interest in apprehending criminals but also suspects' interests in preventing coercive questioning.

Perhaps the most effective replacement for *Miranda* would simply be to videotape or record police interrogations. About one-sixth of all police departments in the country already videotape at least some confessions, and a recent study by the National Institute of Justice concluded that, in addition to providing safeguards for the suspect, videotaping also resulted in the improvement of police interrogation practices, rendered confessions more convincing to judges and juries, and assisted prosecutors in negotiating more favorable plea bargains and guilty pleas. Videotaping would also provide more protection for innocent suspects caught up in the criminal-justice system.

For *Miranda* is not particularly well tailored to protecting a suspect's rights to be free from coercion. Justice John Marshall Harlan's point in his *Miranda* dissent has never been effectively answered: "The new rules are not designed to guard against police brutality or other unmistakably banned forms of coercion. Those who use third-degree tactics and deny them in court are equally able and destined to lie as skillfully about warnings and waivers." It is not clear why police using rubber hoses before

Miranda would have thought it necessary to shelve them afterward. Furthermore, once a valid *Miranda* waiver is obtained, police are relatively free to proceed as they like.

No legacy of the Warren Court has been more devastating to the first civil right of individuals, the right to be protected from attack. Congressional conservatives may choose to place serious procedural reform off-limits. They may do this, in part, because of the burdens of leadership required in order to explain the relationship of procedure to the substantive ability of the justice system to protect society. They may do this because it is easier to deal with public-policy problems whose costs are more visible. However, if effective reform is to be undertaken, unsettling such settled areas of the law as *Miranda* will be required. Until that time, society can do little more than continue to count Justice White's "unknown number" of killers, rapists, and other criminals who go free because of the criminal-justice innovations of the Warren Court.

"Miranda is symbolic of our societal
commitment to the Constitution and
to criminal procedural guarantees."

THE MIRANDA RULE DOES NOT
UNDERMINE THE CRIMINAL JUSTICE
SYSTEM

Susan R. Klein

According to Susan R. Klein, the Miranda rule is a vital hallmark of
the Fifth Amendment and a powerful symbol of society's refusal
to condone constitutional violations. In the following viewpoint,
Klein argues not only that the Miranda rule is necessary to protect
constitutional rights, but also that the Court must strengthen its
commitment to Miranda by imposing harsher penalties for its violation. Further, Klein refutes arguments that the Miranda rule
grossly hinders law enforcement, suggesting that the number of
convictions has not dropped since its implementation. Klein is
assistant professor of law at the University of Texas.

As you read, consider the following questions:

1. In Klein's opinion, why is there a trend among law
   enforcement officials to violate the Miranda rule?
2. How does the author refute the claim that Miranda damages
   law enforcement?
3. According to Klein, how has the Miranda rule contributed to a
   more humane police culture?

Reprinted, with permission, from Susan R. Klein, "Miranda Deconstitutionalized: When the
Self-Incrimination Clause and the Civil Rights Act Collide," University of Pennsylvania Law Review,
vol. 143 (December 1994):417. Copyright ©1994 by the University of Pennsylvania.

The unthinkable happens—you are arrested. You are taken to the police station, put in an interrogation room, and read your rights. We all know them from television by now:

> You have the right to remain silent. If you choose to give up this right, anything you say can and will be used against you in a court of law. You have the right to consult with an attorney, and to have the attorney present during interrogation. If you cannot afford an attorney, one will be appointed to represent you. Do you understand these rights?

Of course you do; you are a law professor, an attorney, a well-informed citizen.

> "I demand to see my lawyer and refuse to answer any questions."
> "Too bad, buddy, we're short on patience today. You're gonna talk to us without your lawyer."
> "What? I demand to see my lawyer!"
> "You have to comply."
> "I'll sue."

(general laughter by officers present)

After hours of nonstop interrogation, one of five possible outcomes emerges: you are guilty and "spill your guts"; you are innocent but confess or make damaging admissions; you are guilty but have the exceptional fortitude to remain quiet; you are innocent and manage to remain silent; you are innocent and eventually convince the police to release you or at least end the interrogation. Except for the first two situations, in which you may have the limited remedy of having your statement excluded from the prosecutor's case-in-chief, there are no remedies available to you for the violation of your so-called "rights.". . .

THE CONSEQUENCES OF ABANDONING MIRANDA

A suspect's "right" to receive her *Miranda* warnings and to have her invocation of the rights contained in those warnings honored has been affirmed in early 1990s court decisions. "Beyond this duty to inform, *Miranda* requires that the police respect the accused's decision to exercise the rights outlined in the warnings. 'If the individual indicates in any manner, at any time prior to or during questioning, that he wishes to remain silent, . . . the interrogation must cease'" [*Moran v. Burbine*]. Likewise, in order to prevent police from badgering a defendant into waiving her previously asserted *Miranda* rights, the Court affirmed that a suspect who has unambiguously invoked her right to counsel cannot be questioned regarding any offense, unless an attorney is actually present. Such rules are necessary to protect the privilege against self-incrimination, otherwise [w]hen a suspect understands his (expressed) wishes to have been ignored . . . in contravention of the 'rights' just read to him by his interrogator, he may well see further objection as futile and confession (true or not) as the only way to end his interrogation" [Davis v. United States].

I believe that few of us would care to live in a society in which police officers could interrogate citizens at will for inde-

---

THE BENEFITS OF MIRANDA

According to University of Chicago professor Stephen Schulhofer, criminal suspects are better off than they were in the due process era because police no longer use physical force or mental coercion to generate confessions. Miranda not only encouraged the police to use more subtle forms of persuasion, it made such ploys more effective. Police learned how to create an interrogation environment where their rendition of the warnings led suspects to believe that they had the power to stop police questioning whenever they wished. Emboldened by this shift in the power-balance, suspects now believe that they can talk their way out of trouble without subjecting themselves to prolonged interrogation and eventual incrimination. Of course they are mistaken, but the Constitution is not offended when criminal suspects make foolish decisions that do not promote their self-interest. Since Miranda does not bar the police from using deceit and trickery to gain suspects' confidence once they have waived their rights, the police are free to play a confidence game in which their eventual betrayal of that trust generates non-coerced incriminating admissions.

Civil libertarians are happy because they get crime control without empowering the state to use the sort of physical or mental coercion that might coerce an innocent person (such as themselves) to confess falsely. Police like Miranda because it provides them with clear guidelines for initiating interrogations and does not eliminate their power to manipulate suspects once they have waived their Miranda rights. Following these guidelines virtually guarantees the admission of any incriminating statement made by criminal suspects. Moreover, police compliance with Miranda demonstrates their commitment to professionalism and respect of suspects' rights. The Supreme Court is happy because the courts are freed from applying a fact-sensitive, labor-intensive, due process test in most of the cases where police complied with Miranda. In sum, Miranda generates benefits to all of the legal actors in the criminal justice system that easily outweigh the relatively insignificant costs of a few lost incriminating admissions.

Peter Arenella, Harvard Journal of Law and Public Policy, Winter 1997.

terminate periods of time (in other words, revert back to pre-*Miranda* "third-degree" police techniques). While it is one thing to be questioned by an attorney or judge in open court (and even be compelled to answer if offered *Kastigar*-type immunity), it is quite another to be interrogated in secret by law enforcement officials. Confession may be "good for the soul" when given to a listener who has your best interests at heart (such as a parent); it is certainly not good for the body when given to those whose utmost desire is to have you incarcerated or executed. This situation creates great harm to the suspect, regardless of whether any statements are ever used against him in a criminal trial. The autonomy and dignity of the individual sought to be protected by the Self-Incrimination Clause is certainly lost.

Although the Court purports to reaffirm the stability and importance of the rights guaranteed by the *Miranda* decision, it has consistently refused to provide an adequate remedy for the violation of these rights. Given the legal obstacles to protecting the Self-Incrimination Clause, an outright disregard for *Miranda*'s safeguards is precisely what is beginning to occur throughout the country. Law enforcement officials are in the business of solving crimes, not protecting constitutional rights. Since the values enshrined in the Self-Incrimination Clause, in certain instances, may not further the truth-seeking function of an investigation and trial, and since these values certainly do not serve the adversarial goals of officers and prosecutors, officers will be tempted to ignore them. Today's Court, by severely limiting the remedies available for violations of the Self-Incrimination Clause and the *Miranda* warnings, not only permits officers to ignore both but actually encourages their violation. . . .

LIMITATIONS ON MIRANDA

If we eliminate *Miranda* entirely, or simply retain its present status as a nonconstitutional prophylactic rule with no effective remedy available for its violation, then police officers can continue to ignore a suspect's request not to be interrogated. In fact, the incentive works in favor of ignoring such a request. There is still an advantage in giving the warnings; if a suspect agrees to waive his rights and gives a confession, that statement might be admissible in the prosecutor's case-in-chief. Once a suspect invokes his rights, however, his subsequent statements become inadmissible anyway, and police officers have nothing to lose by continuing the interrogation and something to gain, such as developing impeachment evidence and other leads. Of course, if the officers break off the interrogation and allow the suspect access to an attorney, the possibility of obtaining a confession are lost.

Thus, there is extreme dissonance between the content of the warnings and the actions of the officers. It is, at best, unseemly for the officers to offer rights which they proceed to ignore. A more honest approach would be to formulate new warnings in light of the limitations on Miranda. For example, the officer might say, "You do not have the right to remain silent. If you request silence or an attorney, the interrogation will continue, but your statements cannot be used against you in the prosecutor's case-in-chief." This statement, however, is not what the Court mandated in Miranda. . . .

MAINTAINING MIRANDA'S SYMBOLIC VALUE

Miranda is symbolic of our societal commitment to the Constitution and to criminal procedural guarantees; it accomplishes this with very little cost in terms of lost convictions. In fact, although a number of studies show a reduction in statements obtained during custodial interrogation immediately following the implementation of the Miranda rules, various other authors refute these statistics. More recent empirical analyses show no decrease in the overall number of convictions. Allowing a federal cause of action under § 1983 for a violation of the Miranda warnings would signify a federal commitment to Fifth Amendment values. In fact, given the permeation of these warnings in American popular culture, a failure to offer a civil rights action itself sends out a loud and definitive message.

CULTURAL MESSAGES

Moreover, this symbolism is not lost on police officers, who, of course, are subject to the same cultural messages as other citizens. As noted by Professor Donald A. Dripps, who is no fan of the privilege:

> [T]he warnings have contributed generally to a more humane police culture, and they surely impose some limits on police tactics in specific cases. The reading of rights affects the questioner, even if it glances off the suspect. Only a corroded conscience could live with reading the Miranda card by the glare of the arc lamp. And the law-abiding police interrogator must tread rather lightly; too much pressure and the suspect may invoke the right to counsel.

Finally, Miranda's exclusionary rule is a symbol of the Court's refusal to condone the unlawful conduct that produced the confession. This "judicial integrity" rationale posits that a court ought to nullify a constitutional violation rather than admit the evidence and thereby permit the government to profit by its wrongdoing. Such denial of court assistance in perpetuating the violation is necessary to maintain respect for the Constitution and to preserve the judicial process.

| "The exclusionary rule makes it more difficult to convict the guilty, including police officers who commit crimes."

THE EXCLUSIONARY RULE WEAKENS THE CRIMINAL JUSTICE SYSTEM

Morgan O. Reynolds

The exclusionary rule falls under the banner of the Fourth Amendment to the Constitution, which prohibits unreasonable searches and seizures by the government. In the following viewpoint, Morgan O. Reynolds argues that the exclusionary rule, which suppresses evidence obtained in violation of the Fourth Amendment, is a barrier to justice. He contends that the law lacks common sense and is so convoluted that even well-intentioned police officers misinterpret it, resulting in thousands of guilty criminals going free each year. Although the law was created in the interest of protecting civil liberties, Reynolds charges that exclusion of evidence does not deter or correct overzealous police searches. Rather, he advocates a repeal of the exclusionary rule, and offers alternative sanctions against police misconduct. Reynolds is director of the Criminal Justice Center of the National Center for Policy Analysis and professor of Economics at Texas A&M University.

As you read, consider the following questions:

1. Why does Reynolds believe that good-faith exceptions to the exclusionary rule are misguided?
2. In the author's opinion, what are alternatives to the exclusionary rule?
3. According to Reynolds, how might the exclusionary rule benefit corrupt police officers?

Reprinted, with permission, from Morgan O. Reynolds, "Why Stop Halfway?" *National Review*, May 15, 1995; ©1995 by National Review, Inc., 215 Lexington Ave., New York, NY 10016.

A motorcycle cop stops a speeding car. Without a search warrant but suspicious, the policeman demands that the driver open his trunk and discovers the corpses of a woman and two children. The man later walks out of court scot-free because the evidence was inadmissible. The criminal's Fourth Amendment rights had been violated.

This miscarriage of justice supposedly improves the protection of our civil liberties, but it does no such thing. The entire theory of suppressing illegally obtained evidence in criminal court is misguided.

The exclusionary rule was concocted by an imaginative Supreme Court in *Weeks* v. *United States* in 1914. Until then, little had been heard about reckless abuse of citizens' constitutional rights by federal law-enforcement officials. The agitated Justices declared that, without their little creature, the Fourth Amendment was "of no value" and "might as well be stricken from the Constitution."

In 1961 Earl Warren and Company initiated their do-good revolution in criminal privileges by imposing the exclusionary rule on all state courts in *Mapp* v. *Ohio*, a breathtaking expansion of power considering that more than 90 per cent of criminal cases are prosecuted by the states. Between 1920 and 1960, half the states had allowed pertinent evidence into criminal proceedings, even if it had allegedly been obtained illegally, on a case-by-case basis. The remaining states, either through statute or through appellate-court decisions, emulated federal suppression. Advocates of quashing had succeeded in twenty states during the 1920s, usually as a device to soften the impact of Prohibition.

A FLAWED DEVICE

Not only does the exclusionary rule have a wholly suspicious origin—the twentieth-century federal judiciary—but it defies common sense and lacks empirical evidence in its favor. As former Chief Justice Warren Burger points out, "There is no empirical evidence to support the claim that the rule actually deters illegal conduct of law-enforcement officials." The exclusionary rule remains unique to American jurisprudence. Our celebrated civil-libertarian neighbor to the north, for example, relies on the tort system to correct overzealous police searches and compensate victims.

Like the rest of the Warren Court revolution, the rule excluding illegally obtained evidence makes so little sense that the courts and Congress have tried steadily to narrow its application. Yet allowing an exception to the exclusionary rule for evidence seized illegally but in good faith is a defective cure. It allows police officers to blunder in good faith again and again. Government agents now routinely conduct unconstitutional searches and seizures with impunity.

Expanding the legal liability of police departments and setting up compensation funds for money damages would make the police respect constitutional liberties and avoid illegal searches and seizures for which they might be sued.

FREEING GUILTY CRIMINALS

The exclusionary rule has benefits only in the eyes of those who judge laws strictly by their intentions rather than their actual effects. The rule offers no civil-liberties benefits, only social cost. It artificially impedes justice by freeing at least 20,000 criminals each year. Statistical studies show that exclusionary rules, all else equal, are associated with a 15 per cent increase in crime rates. The Warren Court has the blood of thousands of crime victims on its hands.

CRIMINALS GOING FREE

If you're looking for the major culprit in the malaise-ridden judicial system, for the kink in the works that practically guarantees justice will not be done, look at the convoluted way the Courts have interpreted the Fourth Amendment. . . .

Few would disagree that in the United States, police officers should not be allowed to just burst into your home, or search your car, or rifle through your handbag on a whim. Such behavior would betray our fundamental right to be protected from unreasonable government interference with our lives. But we've gotten ourselves into a hopeless morass with the Fourth Amendment. Day by day, case by case, the results become more ridiculous and more difficult to understand and predict. The bottom line: Criminals are going free.

I don't mean *alleged* criminals. I'm not referring to *innocent* men and women who were arrested by mistake or because of false evidence. I'm talking about people who are clearly criminals. There's no issue about the reliability of the evidence against them. But that evidence is often completely thrown out because of some technical mistake made in the course of the arrest.

Harold J. Rothwax, *Guilty: The Collapse of Criminal Justice*, 1996.

While most policemen honestly try to follow Fourth Amendment directives, current law is so tortured that even experienced lawyers and judges do not know if particular searches will be upheld by the courts. The exclusionary rule has done more to undermine the Fourth Amendment than to protect it. As District of Columbia Circuit Judge Malcolm Wilkey once wrote: "If one were diabolically to attempt to invent a device designed slowly to undermine the substantive reach of the Fourth Amendment, it would be hard to do better than the exclusionary rule."

The exclusionary rule makes it more difficult to convict the guilty, including police officers who commit crimes. The rule makes it easy for corrupt cops to protect favored criminals from prosecution by simply making an illegal seizure.

The exclusionary rule dooms many criminal prosecutions. Prosecutors have limited budgets and avoid prosecuting cases with serious search and seizure problems. Their reasoning: Why risk a prolonged struggle over the technicalities of the exclusionary rule?

LITTLE PUNITIVE VALUE

The exclusionary rule does not punish overzealous or criminal police conduct because officers and police departments are typically rated on overall arrest clearance rates rather than conviction rates. The police practices attacked by the courts have increased since the do-good rule was imposed nationwide in 1961.

The irony of the exclusionary rule is that the public, not the culpable police, bears the costs of freeing the guilty criminals. Considering the liberal sociological view that "society" is to blame for crime rather than the criminal, this is an ironic success for this theory of justice. Under exclusion of evidence, the criminal freed on a technicality is free to punish society again.

Rather than trying to "gut" the exclusionary rule through good-faith exceptions, it would be better to repeal it in a straightforward way. Montesquieu wrote, "We must not separate the Laws from the End for which they were made." The courts have lost their way, and both they and the public know it. . . . Let's start over. At least allow federalism: let the state legislatures and courts decide whether they want to retain the exclusionary rule or substitute more rational means to make the police respect constitutional liberties.

| "Despite its many flaws, the
exclusionary rule is . . . the best we
can realistically do."

THE EXCLUSIONARY RULE IS NECESSARY

Carol S. Steiker

In the following viewpoint, Carol S. Steiker argues that despite its many flaws, the exclusionary rule plays a vital role in enforcing Fourth Amendment rights and protecting civil liberties. She contends that the middle class is not as likely to be victimized by overzealous police as are the poor or members of minority groups. This racial discrimination in law enforcement, coupled with a pervasive fear of crime in society, fosters widespread public support for unrestrained police power, according to Steiker. In such a climate, and in the absence of other effective constraints against police misconduct, Steiker believes that society must rely on the exclusionary rule to police the police and uphold Fourth Amendment protections. Steiker is assistant professor of law at Harvard Law School.

As you read, consider the following questions:

1. According to the author, what are some of the flaws inherent in the exclusionary rule?
2. Why does Steiker claim that juries will often "fear the robbers more than the cops"?
3. How does the exclusionary rule, in Steiker's opinion, create an alternate vision of "good police work"?

Reprinted, with permission, from Carol S. Steiker, "Second Thoughts About First Principles," *Harvard Law Review*, vol. 107 (February 1994):807.

The exclusionary rule is flawed as a system of deterrence of police misconduct. It awards windfalls to guilty criminal defendants while offering nothing at all to the innocent whose rights are equally violated. It creates skewed litigation incentives, encouraging defendants to pursue even the most unattractive cases and preventing them from seeking the kinds of remedies—for example, injunctions—that might best prevent future violations of the Fourth Amendment. It is not as fine-tuned or "infinitely divisible" a remedy as money damages. And it does have a particularly visible social cost when obviously guilty defendants "get off" on Fourth Amendment "technicalities."

Despite its many flaws, the exclusionary rule is, I am convinced, the best we can realistically do. . . .

A History of Failed Remedies

Almost half a century passed between the recognition of the exclusionary rule in federal prosecutions and the application of the exclusionary rule to the states. During that forty-seven-year period, not one of the majority of states that permitted the evidentiary use of illegally seized evidence managed to create an effective scheme of civil remedies for police misconduct. Indeed, the Supreme Court relied on just this failure when it extended the exclusionary rule to the states in *Mapp v. Ohio*: after noting that California adopted the exclusionary rule on its own because of the failure of other remedies, the Court observed that the "experience of California that such other remedies have been *worthless and futile* is buttressed by the experience of other States." There is no reason to think that the pre-*Mapp* political impediments to the creation of effective alternative remedies have miraculously disappeared. If anything, the escalating public hysteria over violent crime from the 1960s through the present makes it even more "politically suicidal" today to support restrictions on police behavior than it was before 1961.

The problem of racial discrimination in law enforcement helps explain why there is so little public enthusiasm for policing the police. It is simply not the case that the risks of being victimized by malicious or merely overzealous police misconduct fall evenly across the population. As we have seen, the police frequently use race and class as means of targeting individuals for investigation and often subject predominantly minority neighborhoods to particularly intrusive law enforcement techniques. The "average" (meaning not impoverished and not minority) citizen is probably more likely to be a victim of crime than a victim of police overreaching—hence, the willingness of "average" citizens everywhere to give the police a free hand.

This widespread public support for unrestrained police power not only makes the passage of remedial legislation extremely unlikely, it also suggests that, even if such legislation were to be passed, popular juries would be unwilling to find much police conduct "unreasonable.". . . Juries will often fear the robbers more than the cops because the robbers tend to be mostly poor and/or members of minority groups and because the cops tend to focus their attentions on just such disfavored groups. Think of the suburban, middle-class jury from Simi Valley that acquitted the police officers accused of beating motorist Rodney King. Would we really expect such a jury to be a fair arbiter of the "reasonableness" of the sort of police tactics regularly deployed against members of minority groups? And reconsider the repeated trials of the Scottsboro boys in Alabama: local jury after local jury returned death sentences against the defendants, and it was the courts who overturned those verdicts. For the same reasons that we have turned to judges to enforce the anti-majoritarian provisions of the First and Fourteenth Amendments, we must rely upon the judge-made exclusionary rule as the device by which the Fourth Amendment should be enforced. Like it or not, the exclusionary rule, with all of its limitations, is in very real terms "the only game in town."

Because history has shown us again and again that the political process will not create structures that can adequately constrain police misconduct, the exclusionary rule is necessary to enlist the courts in this project. But the exclusionary rule does more than create federal court jurisdiction over Fourth Amendment issues. . . . The exclusionary rule involves the courts in the ongoing project of developing a detailed body of Fourth Amendment law. By creating litigation incentives in a wide body of cases in which defendants will, of necessity, be provided with court-appointed counsel, the exclusionary rule ensures that the courts will develop a fairly comprehensive set of constitutional guidelines for law enforcement—guidelines that the political branches of government would otherwise neglect. If we abandoned the exclusionary rule . . . we would not necessarily see more "sensible" and "straight" discussion of the Fourth Amendment from judges; we instead might hear only a resounding silence.

Some argue that the complex body of law that the Supreme Court and other federal and state courts have constructed around the Fourth Amendment may not, when all is said and done, have much of a deterrent effect on police misconduct.

Many respond to such claims by challenging the underlying empirical assertion. Another common response is that such observations miss the point because the exclusionary rule operates not so much to penalize violations of the Fourth Amendment as to remove the most common incentive for such violations—the discovery of evidence to be used to convict a criminal defendant. Yet the debate about deterrent effects may miss the point in a much more profound way: the body of constitutional law developed by exclusionary rule litigation may be important not so much for the fear that it inspires in the "bad cop," but rather in the way that it creates an alternative vision of the "good cop."

A Check on Judicial Power

Any system that regulates evidence gathering lets some armed robbers and drug dealers get away with their crimes. That is automatically true whenever the law limits what the police can look at, indeed whenever the law in any way raises the cost of gathering evidence. The difference between the exclusionary rule and, say, a damages remedy for Fourth Amendment violations (again, taking the content of Fourth Amendment law as a given) is not that the exclusionary rule prevents some robbers from being caught—a damages remedy does that too—but that the exclusionary rule shines a spotlight on a few of the robbers and drug dealers who go free. The criminals who get away because the police didn't bother to get a warrant are not invisible. We see them, at least sometimes.

The exclusionary rule's critics think this fact undermines our faith in the criminal justice system. To some degree they are probably right, though there are plenty of other reasons for the public's lack of faith in the system. But the critics ignore the other side of the coin. Whatever its costs, the visibility of the criminal who walks away has an important benefit: it makes *courts* see the consequences of the constitutional rules they create for the police. This is no small matter. To a degree unsurpassed around the world, the United States has given judges (more precisely, judges have given themselves) the job of writing and enforcing the rules that cover day-to-day criminal law enforcement. . . . Even if this institutional arrangement is necessary, it creates the potential for bad lawmaking. The exclusionary rule is a useful check on that potential, a way of limiting counter-majoritarian excess. Judges who write rules that prevent the capture of the occasional rapist are forced to see an occasional rapist walk away as a result of those rules. And the rest of us can see it, too. That may serve to rein in overly aggressive judicial lawmakers.

William J. Stuntz, *Harvard Journal of Law and Public Policy*, Winter 1997.

Our modern police forces have developed a separate culture that rewards highly aggressive attitudes and behavior patterns, a culture that has proven largely impervious to outside influence. The development of an alternative vision of "good police work" founded on such a fundamental text as the Constitution offers "good cops" guidance in defining their mission and thus provides an aspirational counterpart to the internal ethos of local police departments.

PERIODICAL BIBLIOGRAPHY

The following articles have been selected to supplement the diverse views presented in this chapter. Addresses are provided for periodicals not indexed in the *Readers' Guide to Periodical Literature*, the *Alternative Press Index*, the *Social Sciences Index*, or the *Index to Legal Periodicals and Books*.

Akhil Reed Amar	"The Future of Constitutional Criminal Procedure," *American Criminal Law Review*, Summer 1996. Available from 600 New Jersey Ave. NW, Washington, DC 20001.
Peter Arenella	"Miranda Stories," *Harvard Journal of Law and Public Policy*, Winter 1997. Available from William S. Hein & Co., Inc., 1285 Main Street, Buffalo, NY 14209.
Robert E. Bauman	"Congress and the Exclusionary Rule," *National Review*, May 15, 1995.
Mark Clayton	"Captives of Flawed Justice Systems," *Christian Science Monitor*, March 27, 1995. Available from One Norway St., Boston, MA 02115.
Roger Cossack	"Are Too Many Guilty Defendants Going Free?" *American Criminal Law Review*, Summer 1996.
Edward M. Hendrie	"Beyond Miranda," *FBI Law Enforcement Bulletin*, March 1997.
Richard A. Leo	"Inside the Interrogation Room," *Journal of Criminal Law and Criminology*, Winter 1996. Available from Northwestern University School of Law, 357 E. Chicago Ave., Chicago, IL 60611.
William T. Pizzi	"Punishment and Procedure: A Different View of the American Criminal Justice System," *Constitutional Commentary*, Summer 1995. Available from University of Minnesota Law School, 229 19th Ave. South, Minneapolis, MN 55455.
Nina Totenberg	"Do Criminal Defendants Have Too Many Rights?" *American Criminal Law Review*, Summer 1996.
Gregory J. Wallance	"The Exclusionary Rule's Price to Society Is Too High," *Wall Street Journal*, January 25, 1995.

CHAPTER 3

WHAT SENTENCING LAWS SHOULD GUIDE THE CRIMINAL JUSTICE SYSTEM?

CHAPTER PREFACE

One of the most heavily debated issues in the criminal justice system is who should go to prison and for how long. It seems that no matter what procedures are proposed to make sentencing consistent and fair, critics charge that the solutions are arbitrary, fickle, and disparate. One such solution is statutory mandatory minimum sentencing. These laws attempt to eliminate judicial discretion in sentencing by requiring judges to impose fixed sentences for particular crimes. Since 1980, every state has enacted laws mandating minimum prison sentences, and today over one hundred federal laws specify mandatory minimum sentences for certain crimes, such as drug trafficking or firearm violations.

Those who support mandatory minimums point to unwarranted sentencing disparities resulting from myriad factors, ranging from a judge's personal beliefs and background to the characteristics of the offender, including criminal history, race, or even gender. Advocates of mandatory minimums praise the laws for eliminating these factors from sentencing considerations: Under mandatory minimums, people convicted of comparable offenses receive similar punishments. Many advocates maintain too that tough sentencing policies benefit society by incapacitating criminals. Mandatory minimum sentencing, they maintain, carries the threat of lengthy punishment, a key weapon in the fight against crime. A common criticism of mandatory minimums is that these laws unfairly target nonviolent drug dealers. Advocates dismiss these claims. According to Texas Republican Phil Gramm, "The violence that drug dealers inflict on society is massive. . . . It is just and proper that the punishment society metes out to such 'nonviolent' drug criminals is swift, certain and severe."

Critics charge that mandatory minimum sentencing is unfair, overly rigid, and that eliminating the judge's role in sentencing has resulted in injustice. They argue that mandatory minimums often result in wholly disproportionate sentences. Opponents commonly cite the case of Angela Thomas as an example of how mandatory minimums can result in unfair sentencing: Thomas spent her childhood being raised by relatives, including an uncle who was a major drug dealer. At his direction, seventeen-year-old Thomas—who had never been in trouble with the law—sold an undercover officer two ounces of cocaine. Under mandatory minimum sentencing, Thomas was sentenced to fifteen years to life in prison. The judge was not allowed to consider that Thomas's uncle had masterminded the sale, or even that she lacked a criminal record. Jerome W. Marks, a retired New York City Supreme Court justice, observed, "This is one of the great injustices that I've run across. I was a judge for twenty-two years and I never had a case where a youngster seventeen years of age, with no criminal background at all, ends up doing fifteen years to life." Other critics point to cases in which convicted killers received lighter sentences than Angela Thomas's fifteen years to life. They argue that such disparities prove that mandatory minimums lack any semblance of balance.

In the following chapter, the authors debate the merits and pitfalls of various sentencing strategies.

| "Washington State's experience has shown that [a Three Strikes] law is both effective and affordable."

"THREE STRIKES" LAWS CAN REDUCE CRIME

David LaCourse Jr.

In 1993, Washington was the first state to pass a "three strikes" law that mandates a twenty-five-year-to-life sentence for anyone convicted of a third felony defined as serious or violent. Since then, many other states and the federal government have followed Washington's lead, enacting similar versions of "three strikes" laws aimed at repeat, violent criminals. David LaCourse Jr., who helped draft Washington's "three strikes" initiative, argues in the following viewpoint that these laws are a fair, effective, and affordable approach to combating crime. Lacourse asserts that Washington's experience proves that "three strikes" laws can work. The Washington law has played a key role in reducing crime because it targets habitual criminal activity and acts as a deterrent. LaCourse is the executive director of Washington Citizens for Justice and is a former research analyst for the Washington Institute for Policy Studies.

As you read, consider the following questions:

1. According to LaCourse, how does the "three strikes" law actually target four- and five-strike crimes?
2. According to the author, what anecdotal evidence suggests that "three strikes" laws are effective deterrents?
3. What does the high percentage of criminals sentenced to life without parole for robbery suggest about enforcement of Washington's "three strikes" law, in LaCourse's opinion?

Reprinted from R. David LaCourse Jr., "'Three Strikes, You're Out': A Review," a publication of the Washington Institute for Policy Studies, February 1997, by permission of the institute.

In 1993, Washington was the first state in the nation to pass a no-nonsense *Three Strikes* policy. Since then 23 other states and the federal government have enacted some form of *Three Strikes, You're Out* laws to deal with repeat serious criminals. . . .

CRIMES PREVENTED

After *Three Strikes* passed, initiative supporters expected to sentence not only people with three separate convictions for serious crimes, but also four-time and even five-time violent criminals. The following 'four- and five-strike' crimes would have been prevented if Washington State had enacted *Three Strikes* sooner.

Michael Elton Johnson was one of the first people sentenced under *Three Strikes*. Strike One was a 1976 second-degree rape in Montana, in which Johnson dragged a 14-year-old girl into the woods and raped her. Within a few weeks of his release in 1980, Johnson committed Strike Two for an attempted second-degree rape of a 15-year-old girl in the Wenatchee area during a burglary.

His Strike Three for second-degree assault was perpetrated just a month after his release from prison in 1991. During this attack, Johnson cut his wife's face and neck, rammed a 9-inch-bladed knife into her mouth, pointed a pellet gun at her head and told her that he "would kill her anytime" he wished. At this time, *Three Strikes* was only a concept, so instead of receiving a life-without-parole sentence for the brutal assault, he received only a two-year sentence.

Immediately after his release, Michael Johnson returned to preying on women and children. He was arrested for domestic violence and malicious mischief in Snohomish County for again beating his wife, who finally divorced him. Shortly after that, the Department of Corrections was informed that Johnson had been caught following a 17-year-old girl into a ferry-boat restroom in Snohomish County. Johnson subsequently moved to Oregon briefly, where he raped his own sister and threatened her life before moving back to eastern Washington. He was also charged with fourth-degree assault for putting a woman in a headlock after going into a tavern with her. She escaped unharmed, but was terrified by the experience.

Johnson then befriended a Springdale woman who lived with her 16-year-old daughter. On Christmas Day, 1993, he committed Strike Four by raping the daughter and kidnapping both her and her mother and taking them to a neighboring county. The next day he raped the daughter again before releasing them both. He pleaded guilty to two counts of rape and one count of kidnapping. The other kidnapping charge, the rape of his sister, and the non-Strike assaults were all dropped in exchange for his guilty plea.

In 1994 Michael Elton Johnson was sentenced to life without parole under *Three Strikes*. Michael Johnson's last three rapes, two kidnappings and four other assaults would have been prevented if *Three Strikes* had been enacted just three years earlier. . . .

Martin T. Shandel is actually a five-striker specializing in rape. Strike One was for sexually assaulting a 14-year-old girl in 1967. He was paroled in 1969.

Shandel's Strike Two was for raping a 13-year-old girl who was walking home along a country road in 1971. He stopped his car, forced her into a wooded area and raped her. Just an hour before the attack, he had grabbed two younger girls and attempted, but failed, to force them into his car.

His Strike Three was for second-degree assault with a knife. He forced a woman off the road, brandished a knife and broke out her car window. He then grabbed her arm but was scared off by a witness.

His predatory behavior would have been stopped at this point by *Three Strikes*, had it been in effect. It wasn't, and Shandel was paroled yet again just six years later.

His Strike Four was for raping a 37-year-old woman whose home he was visiting in 1985. He attacked her after she asked him to leave. This last rape occurred just three months after his most recent release.

This victim sued the Washington State Department of Corrections for failing to adequately supervise Shandel. She was awarded $204,000 by a King County Superior Court jury in 1992. The state appealed the decision and the State Court of Appeals overturned the award on a technicality. The State Supreme Court then reinstated the monetary award and the victim finally has received it.

Martin Shandel was released yet again in 1994. Less than a year later, he committed Strike Five for the second-degree rape of his sister-in-law at the Woodinville home he shared with his wife in 1995. His reign of terror ended when he was convicted under the new *Three Strikes* law and sentenced to life without parole.

While these . . . criminals represent the kind of monstrous predators most people wanted stopped under *Three Strikes*, there is another category of criminal that was targeted—the chronic street thug committing robbery and assault over and over again. Far too many of them also continue violence beyond three convictions. . . .

Dwight Anthony Griffin is [one example of a chronic] persistent street criminal. Strike One was for 3 robberies in 1975 of a tavern, a hair salon and a service station. In each case, Griffin told his victims that he had a gun, but did not display it. Instead, he kept one hand in his coat where it appeared that his hand was on a weapon. Griffin was also suspected in two other robberies but was not convicted for them.

His Strike Two was for second-degree robbery in 1980 of another gas station.

Griffin's Strike Three was for second-degree robbery of a knitting shop in 1986. But he didn't stop there.

Strike Four was in 1989 for 4 robberies in the second degree: a donut shop, a service station, a hair salon and a food company. In each robbery, Griffin claimed to have a gun, and in at least one, he threatened to "blow away" a victim.

Strike Five was for attempted robbery in the second degree in 1994. He jumped a woman who was walking to her bank carrying a cash deposit bag. When she refused to give up the money, Griffin knocked her to the ground and began striking her and beating her head into the ground.

Dwight Griffin's crime sprees ended with this violent act because he was sentenced to life without parole under Three Strikes. . . .

The pain, injury and fear that these criminals inflicted upon their victims and their victims' families is immeasurable. And this total doesn't include the non-Strike felonies and misdemeanor crimes committed by these offenders. In addition, there is no way to know how many crimes this group committed that remain unsolved or were not even reported to the police.

These . . . criminals are not the only four- and five-strike felons who have been sentenced under Washington's Three Strikes law, but they are a good representation of the kinds of criminals that the law is capturing. As a result of Three Strikes, Washington State will see fewer of these four- and five-strike offenders in the future.

Washington's Three Strikes law became enforceable on December 2, 1993, one month after voters passed the initiative into law. . . .

From 1993–1995, violent crime dropped 4.8%, in spite of the fact that property crimes increased 8.2% during the same time period. When adjusted for Washington's population growth, a 3.6% increase, the violent crime rate plummeted 8.1% while property crimes rose 4.4%.

Putting these figures another way, there were 256 fewer rapes, 171 fewer robberies and 845 fewer assaults in 1995 than in 1993. While it is too early to prove cause and effect—that Three Strikes legislation reduced violent crime—the recent crime trend is promising. The fact that violent crime decreased, especially in the face of a general crime increase for all other categories, is very encouraging.

In addition, anecdotal evidence clearly indicates that at least some criminals have altered their behavior because of Washington's law.

Many police officers, corrections officers and others, both inside and outside the criminal justice system, have noted that criminals fear *Three Strikes*. These people have also found that some criminals have modified their behavior. For once, felons are worried about the criminal justice system and that has proven to be a deterrent factor.

Some of the more extensive records have been kept by Detective Bob Shilling, who is in charge of the sex-offender detail of the special assault unit for the Seattle Police Department.

Between the time when *Three Strikes* first made the ballot and its election-day victory, Detective Shilling recorded that 17 two-strike (or worse) sex offenders fled to other states from Seattle alone.

In addition, more than 42 Seattle sex offenders called with questions and concerns about which crimes were listed as strikes and whether their priors counted as strikes.

In the week following the passage of *Three Strikes*, Detective Shilling met with three sex offenders, all two-strikers. The first sex offender complained that it wasn't fair that he already had two strikes against him. The other two sex offenders sought treatment for the first time in their lives and wanted Detective Shilling's help in finding a program. Both stated their fear of a life-without-parole sentence under *Three Strikes*. More important, neither has re-offended to date. . . .

Washington's *Three Strikes* law is narrowly focused—it affects only violent, career criminals who show no sign of stopping their violent ways. Research showed that only a few career criminals could be covered under the proposal since only about 12% of all state felonies and felony circumstances were included as strikes. Both the Washington Institute and the state's own Sentencing Guidelines Commission (SGC) estimated that out of more than 16,500 felony sentences handed down yearly, only 60-75 career criminals would qualify under Washington's *Three Strikes* law.

The SGC also did a "worst case" estimate on the prison-bed impact of *Three Strikes*. Since violent career criminals were already sentenced to prison terms, most for between 5–20 years before *Three Strikes*, the effect on prison population would not occur until 5–20 years later when felons are not released as scheduled because of *Three Strikes*.

After 20 years, the state expected a total increase of 885 inmates, or a 9% increase over 1992 levels. This estimate will have to be dramatically lowered since only 83 criminals have been sentenced under the law after just over three years (December 2, 1993–December 20, 1996). This is about one-third of the expected total.

Many factors contribute to such a huge difference in the actual-versus-expected figures. One of these reasons, as indicated above, is that there has been a deterrent factor on the targeted group of violent, career criminals. This deterrent effect should increase in the future. Not only are first- and second-time inmates meeting career criminals who have been sentenced to life without parole under the law, but prosecutors and judges have started warning strike-one and strike-two offenders as to what sentence occurs after the third conviction for such a crime.

Of the 83 three-strikers, 45% were robbers, 20% were sex offenders and 13% were serious assaulters (for their last conviction). An additional 10% were murderers, while 6% were kidnappers, 5% were armed/violent burglars, and an arsonist accounted for 1%. These numbers are similar to the state's estimates with the exception of robbers and sex offenders. The initial estimates predicted 34% for robbers and 26% for sex offenders.

This unexpectedly high percentage of three-strikers sentenced to life without parole for robbery is an encouraging sign that prosecutors are not shying away from enforcing the law as a mandatory sentence. Unarmed robbery was the one crime that initiative backers were concerned that prosecutors might plead down to a non-Strike crime to avoid a trial and guarantee a conviction. The fact that 24% of all three-strikers were last convicted of either attempted or completed robbery in the second degree provides overwhelming evidence that this is not true. Therefore, the smaller-than-expected number of three-strikers cannot be dismissed as due to any lack of enforcement in Washington State.

Aside from much lower numbers of three-strikers, Washington's Three Strikes law has worked as intended. The law is incarcerating violent, career criminals who are unlikely to change their behavior. This is evidenced by the fact that for the 83 three-strikers sentenced to date, their average age is 37 years old. . . .

Three Strikes will remain popular with voters and unpopular with violent, career criminals. As more states examine either adding or modifying their career-criminal statutes, they should turn to the Washington State model for guidance. Washington State's experience has shown that such a law is both effective and affordable.

| "Is it just to sentence an individual to twenty-five years to life for a minor offense?"

"THREE STRIKES" LAWS ARE INCONSISTENT AND OVERLY PUNITIVE

Joseph D. McNamara

In the following viewpoint, Joseph D. McNamara argues that, as currently mandated, "three strikes" laws are riddled with problems. Foremost, McNamara maintains, "three strikes" laws often do not distinguish between violent and nonviolent offenders. Imposing a twenty-five-year-to-life sentence on nonviolent, petty criminals is unfair, inappropriate, and does little to enhance public safety, in McNamara's opinion. While proponents of the legislation cite a decrease in crime, he points out that these lower crime rates may not be directly attributable to "three strikes." These laws are unsound economically, McNamara continues, because law violators will continue to clog an already overburdened prison system. McNamara is a research fellow at the Hoover Institution and the former chief of police of Kansas City, Missouri, and San Jose, California.

As you read, consider the following questions:

1. According to McNamara, what percentage of nonviolent offenders are sentenced under "three strikes" laws?
2. In the author's opinion, why has the number of new trials increased dramatically under "three strikes" laws?
3. Why does McNamara believe that voters are becoming somewhat more moderate in their stance against crime?

Reprinted from Joseph D. McNamara, "The Costs of Getting Tough," *Hoover Digest*, no. 3, 1997, which was adapted from McNamara, "Criminal Justice: The Hottest Hot Button," in *Governing the Golden State*, edited by Gerald C. Lubenow and Bruce E. Cain (Berkeley: Governmental Studies Press, 1997), by permission of the Regents of the University of California.

It is fair to say that a single crime committed in 1993 has shaped the size and functions of California's huge criminal justice network for the rest of the century and beyond.

At approximately 10:30 p.m. on October 1, 1993, twelve-year-old Polly Klaas was taken at knife point from her bedroom by Richard Allen Davis, an ex-convict twice convicted of kidnapping as well as other sex crimes. When Davis was identified as a suspect, a great deal of news coverage focused on his record of violence. Approximately two months after the crime, Davis was arrested and eventually told the police where he had buried the little girl's body after sexually assaulting her. It angered millions of people that this pretty youngster had been taken from the supposed safety of her bedroom by a criminal most people believed should never have been released from prison.

THREE STRIKES ENACTED

The case fueled growing public fear of crime and perceived lenient treatment of violent criminals. As a result, in March 1994 "three strikes" legislation was passed with bipartisan support in California. Eight months later, California voters overwhelmingly passed Proposition 184, a ballot initiative similar to the original three strikes law and equally punitive. During the same period, twenty-two other states passed similar laws and Congress enacted comparable legislation for federal crimes.

The slogan "three strikes and you're out" was used to advocate the law, which requires a life sentence for a third felony conviction if a previous felony was serious or contained elements of violence. Under the three strikes law, the new felony need not be serious or violent and the previous conviction could have occurred in another state or as a juvenile offense if the defendant had been, at the time of the previous offense, sixteen or younger. The law also calls for doubling the sentence on a second felony conviction if it or the prior conviction was serious or violent. Judges are required to give the severest sentence. At least 80 percent of the sentence must be served regardless of good behavior or work time credit. The three strikes law was passed in California as an emergency act. Any amendment will require a two-thirds vote of the legislature.

Clearly, most Californians, like most Americans, were unimpressed that national crime rates had been decreasing since 1992. Voters were sending a strong message of impatience with violent crime. Yet there are unintended consequences to establishing public policies on an emotional basis.

A 1996 study showed that, under the three strikes law, "more than twice as many marijuana possessors (192) had been sentenced for second and third strikes in California as for murder (4), rape (25), and kidnapping (24)." In other words, 85 percent of all offenders sentenced under a law that was intended to punish violence were sentenced instead for nonviolent offenses.

Another study found that "the law was intended to send a clear message to repeat criminals. But no one agrees what the message is." The study, of all fifty-eight counties in California, found that the law was being interpreted differently by politicians, judges, defense attorneys, and prosecutors. San Diego prosecuted vigorously under the law. Los Angeles County did likewise, contributing almost 40 percent of the 2,058 inmates incarcerated under three strikes provisions as of June 1996. Alameda County was more selective, as was San Francisco County, which sent only eighteen three strikes felons to prison. Kern County sent almost ten times more people per capita to prison under three strikes than did Alameda County.

TARGETING NONVIOLENT OFFENDERS

Unexpected problems are already cropping up in the states that have "three strikes" laws. Take the case of Steven Drake Gordon, who holds the dubious distinction of being the first person in Sacramento to be prosecuted under "three strikes and you're out." Addicted to drugs and homeless for the past nine years, Gordon had a record typical of small-time crooks: a few charges of drug possession, disturbing the peace, resisting arrest, and two convictions for theft. In 1986, Gordon took $200 out of the cash register of a fast food joint in New York. Five years later, Gordon stole a woman's purse in Sacramento. In neither crime did Gordon act violently in any way.

But on March 8, 1994, the morning after Governor Pete Wilson signed "three strikes and you're out" into California law, Gordon stole a wallet that contained $100 from a bicyclist. He had struck out. Under the new law, Gordon, as a three-time felon, faced 25 years to life in prison: roughly three times the sentence a convicted murderer would serve.

Suddenly "three strikes and you're out" didn't look as fail-safe as Californians had thought.

Daniel Franklin, *Washington Monthly*, September 1994.

In San Francisco, District Attorney Terrance Hallinan refused to count a drug felony as a third strike. In another county, however, the district attorney prosecuted a defendant for possessing a few grams of cocaine. In one of the first three strikes cases, the victim herself nullified the prosecution by refusing to press charges. The defendant had stolen her bicycle from an open garage (a "serious" felony burglary under California law). The victim felt that the thief should be punished but that it was unjust to sentence someone to twenty-five years for stealing a bicycle.

Three strikes has increased the number of inmates jailed before and after trial. Mandatory sentences of twenty-five years and life mean that prisons increasingly will need expanded health care for inmates seventy and eighty years old. The California Department of Corrections, asserting in 1995 that the prison system was at 180 percent of capacity and that fifteen new prisons would need to be constructed at a cost of $4.5 billion, predicted a 70 percent increase in California's prison population.

In addition, the number of new trials has increased dramatically because defense attorneys are often unwilling to allow a client to plead guilty even to a first felony since subsequent convictions will be punished so much more severely. If it is a second or third felony charge liable under three strikes, the punishment is so harsh that the defendant will most likely seek a trial even when evidence of guilt seems overwhelming.

THE UNCLEAR IMPACT ON CRIME

Supporters of three strike provisions complained that a combination of plea bargaining and lenient sentencing by judges allowed convicted criminals to return to society, where they frequently would commit further violence. Yet two years after three strikes laws became effective, plea bargaining and disparate sentencing are still prevalent in California.

Moreover, the effects of three strikes laws on crime are vigorously disputed. The governor and attorney general contend that the laws reduced crime in California because they resulted in the imprisonment of more than fifteen thousand repeat felons—approximately fourteen thousand on second strike and thirteen hundred on third strike convictions.

On the other hand, the independent legislative analyst for California pointed out that crime had been declining in California for two years *before* the passage of three strikes laws. Other analysts argue that there has been a decline in crime throughout the United States related to a decrease in the number of males in high-crime age groups (fourteen to twenty-four years of age) and a decrease in unemployment. They insist that the decreases in California's crime rate cannot be attributed to the new sentencing regulations.

The social scientists Gottfredson and Hirschi similarly reject the notion that huge increases in penal incapacitation in California produced lower crime rates. Having reviewed the literature on theories of criminality, they conclude that "we are treating many low-rate offenders as though they were high-rate offenders." They, like a number of other social scientists, also raise the ethical issue of unfairness implicit in three strikes sentencing. Is it just to sentence an individual to twenty-five years to life for a minor offense? Many offenses, such as breaking into an automobile to steal property, would not be a felony in other states. The rationale used to justify these harsh sentences is that the offender might commit other, more serious crimes in the future. The preponderance of research, however, indicates that criminality decreases with age and that it is not possible to predict future criminal behavior in the case of any given individual. Ethical questions also arise over the legislative analyst's finding that 60 to 70 percent of those prosecuted under three strikes are black or Hispanic.

The kidnapping of Polly Klaas was a statistical rarity. In 1994 only 2,232 arrests for kidnapping occurred in California, or .135 percent of the total 1,652,723 arrests. Kidnapping is not a common crime. Yet the poignancy of the Polly Klaas case is undeniable and the rage and the fear of the voters understandable.

There is no reason to expect media coverage of crime, public fear, and the response of those running for public office to change. Jury nullifications, the passage of Proposition 215 (the Medical Marijuana Act), and the defeat of a proposition to fund the building of more jails in the November 1996 election may be signs that voters are becoming somewhat more moderate in their inclinations toward harsh sentences. Nevertheless, modifying the California three strikes provisions will require that two-thirds of the legislature and the governor expose themselves to potential accusations of being soft on crime. Unless the courts intervene on constitutional grounds, it is likely that massive incarceration of law violators will continue in California for years to come. One analysis estimates that, over the next seven years, the cost of running prisons will rise from 9 percent of the state's general funds to 18 percent.

Eventually, tensions will develop as criminal justice expenditures require increased taxes or divert so much revenue from schools and other public programs that voters will consider sending a different message to those whom they elect.

> "Passage of mandatory sentencing laws vents and wastes public anger without furthering the goal of that anger— effective action against crime."

MANDATORY MINIMUM SENTENCING SHOULD BE ABOLISHED

Vincent L. Broderick

In the last decade, Congress and various state legislatures have enacted mandatory minimum sentencing laws which impose sentences based on a statutory description of a crime, without factoring in any mitigating circumstances. In the following viewpoint, Vincent L. Broderick argues that mandatory minimum sentencing laws are unjust, ineffective, counterproductive, and weaken the criminal justice system. According to Broderick, political figures—posturing to appear "tough on crime"—support the use of mandatory sentences because they have great superficial appeal as a potent weapon against crime. Broderick contends that while the public's fear of crime and violence may be justified, mandatory minimum sentencing is not an anti-crime panacea. Vincent L. Broderick is a judge of the U.S. District Court for the Southern District of New York.

As you read, consider the following questions:

1. According to the author, why was the first experiment with mandatory sentencing in the 1960s unsuccessful?
2. In Broderick's opinion, what is the danger in allowing prosecutors to use plea bargaining in conjunction with mandatory minimum sentencing?
3. What mitigating factors merit departure from mandatory minimum sentencing, according to Broderick?

Reprinted from Vincent L. Broderick, "The Delusion of Mandatory Sentencing: The Wrong Approach to Fighting Crime," Trial, August 1994, by permission of the publisher.

Public distress concerning crime has justifiably reached a crescendo, calling on the law enforcement community to devise effective means to promote fair and effective law enforcement. For reasons described below, mandatory minimum sentencing is not such a means. The judiciary is virtually unanimous on that point, permitting me to testify before the Subcommittee on Crime of the House Judiciary Committee on July 28, 1993, "I am here to express the complete and unmitigated opposition of the federal judges of this country to mandatory minimums."

Counterproductive panaceas such as mandatory minimum sentencing can only be overcome if wise solutions are suggested as alternatives—even if they are controversial and require further discussion. Alternative means must include more effective methods of investigation, not relying on use of unreliable informants or confessions during coercive interrogation but using other options that can and must be developed. Alternatives must include corrections that discourage irresponsible behavior and encourage growth of responsibility while one is in prison. They may well include an expanded role of citizen self-defense against crime. And perhaps most crucial of all, they must involve challenging jobs that would permit productive elements of society to compete with criminal elements for the allegiance of new members of that society.

Recognizing the urgency of anticrime efforts, we should examine the helpful or harmful role of mandatory sentencing laws. I am convinced that mandatory sentencing represents a siren song for legislators and candidates for office because it gives a false appearance of promoting the following important goals:

• to take an effective step toward combating crime, particularly violent crime;
• to combat revolving-door justice; and
• to prevent use of undue leniency as a device to move court calendars.

Mandatory sentencing furthers none of these objectives. Passage of mandatory sentencing laws vents and wastes public anger without furthering the goal of that anger—effective action against crime. In fact, these laws paradoxically impede rather than promote effective law enforcement practices.

Mandatory minimum sentencing does nothing to increase the likelihood that a criminal will be tracked down, arrested, or convicted. To the contrary, during the first experiment with mandatory sentencing in the 1960s, limited at that time to narcotics offenses, the number of reversals on procedural grounds spurted up because of distaste for harsh sentences against minor offenders. Recognizing the futility of the mandatory sentence as an antidote to crime, Congress repealed the law in 1970.

Even a rule that after a certain number of "strikes" (violent crimes) a malefactor is permanently incarcerated—or, as the British call it, "potted"—is delusionary. Most violent criminals escape arrest or conviction.

Moreover, not all crimes are equally unprovoked. Both courts and juries become reluctant to convict if sympathy is generated by any extenuating circumstances—if, for example, a person strikes out against a fleeing criminal or an abusive spouse. The same members of the public who call for blood as citizens often acquit obviously guilty defendants if a sympathy factor, however delusionary, can be injected into the proceedings. Pretending that folklore fails to inform jurors about the consequences of verdicts is tunnel vision at its most myopic.

LETTING CRIMINALS WALK FREE

It is also naive to believe that mandatory minimums keep criminals locked up. As put by one legal commentator, "Where mandatory penalties are perceived as inappropriately severe, the legal system will try, subject to institutional constraints, to prevent or reduce the frequency of their imposition."

Mandatory minimum sentencing increases the tendency of prison authorities or political decisionmakers—who would have to find money to deal with more and more prisoners—to tell judicial administrators, police, prosecutors, and judges that they must find ways to release many dangerous offenders because of prison overcrowding. According to some frequently denied but reliably reported information, judges in quite a few jurisdictions are ordered informally to give a certain number of "free walks" to a narcotics peddler before considering imprisonment.

It is an equally dangerous myth that mandatory minimums avoid unduly lenient sentences. Instead, the decision for leniency is merely moved to the earlier plea bargaining phase. Although statistically it may not appear that criminals are sentenced lightly for heinous offenses, the criminal so favored is never charged with the offense actually committed but with a lesser one. The incentives for this sleight of hand are twofold.

COERCING DEFENDANTS

First, some prosecutors use the carrot of a lighter charge combined with the stick of the mandatory minimum associated with a realistic charge to coerce defendants into "cooperating" with the authorities. Often the most serious offenders are induced to report on or testify against others who may or may not be guilty. This improves the statistical catch of law enforcement and reduces the effort needed for independent investigation and prosecutorial evaluation of the facts.

Second, plea bargaining to move court calendars—despite its drawback in coercing pleas by defendants who may not be guilty and rewarding worse offenders willing to "cooperate"— is difficult or impossible to eradicate, certainly by fiat. However, the practice of using these enticements is often less necessary than assumed. A defendant may benefit by avoiding having a trial place the details of the crime graphically before the sentencing judge. This means a defendant has an inherent incentive to plead guilty to the original charge to avoid trial and hope for a lesser sentence.

"Personally I like you, but the mood of the country dictates that I stick it to you good."

Parading evidence of a crime before the sentencer is a far more potent promoter of substantial sentences than paper minimums, which can readily be avoided by dismissing the case on one ground or another if the result is sufficiently offensive to the trial or appellate court. Use of this natural deterrent to frivolous insistence on trials where there is no defense avoids the many nefarious aspects of the current reliance on bargaining to clear court dockets.

Mandatory minimum sentencing, on the other hand, requires plea bargaining as the only way to avoid imposing excessive sentences on minor offenders. At the same time, it creates an often irresistible temptation for prosecutors to use the stick of potential minimum periods of incarceration to forcibly recruit informants or cooperating witnesses of dubious credibility.

HARMFUL SIDE EFFECTS

Mandatory sentencing hurts effective law enforcement by wasting jail space where minor malefactors happen to meet a wooden textual description of an offense. This phenomenon occurs when numerical factors of crimes determine sentences. For example, one may be far more dangerous brandishing a weapon that adds merely a short time to one's sentence while stealing $10 from a bank than when entering a safe to steal $1 million. Yet the latter offender receives the harsher penalty. A sophisticated drug operative caught with one-tenth of an ounce of a controlled substance may be far more hazardous to society than a lower-echelon carrier of 10 ounces, but the carrier is punished more severely.

Indeed, minor offenders can be ruined for life. A peripheral figure pressured or duped into participating in an illegal activity may meet statutory criteria for commission of a crime calling for lengthy mandatory imprisonment. The results may include not merely loss of time, worthwhile opportunities, and ability to meet family responsibilities; they may include inability to obtain future employment, development of lifelong resentment, and acquisition of criminal skills in a taxpayer-supported school for crime.

Less obviously but just as surely, mandatory sentencing denigrates the independence of the judiciary, which is treated as a robotic rather than intelligent branch of government. Indeed, one distinguished state jurist resigned rather than obey an appellate mandate to implement a wooden minimum.

Such sentencing also deprives the court of options that may lead to rehabilitation, such as ordering the defendant to go to "boot camp," leave the area, or submit to close supervision by family or other trusted people. This kind of rigidity is based on the unexamined assumption that the statutory description of a crime contains all the information needed for wise disposition of the offender—a form of what Justice Oliver Wendell Holmes, Jr., called "delusive exactness."

The weed dies hard, however, because it has superficial appeal. It gives the public a false sense that something effective is being done about crime, diverting attention from meaningful steps that urgently need to be taken. These include developing more effective means of law enforcement and dealing with underlying factors like the lack of adequate job opportunities for many who are attracted by criminal gangs or syndicates. These important issues take the back seat to misinformed crusading for tough mandatory sentencing.

COMBATING THE EVIL

The simplest means of extirpating the bane of mandatory sentencing is the direct one used by Congress in 1970 when it repealed the first mandatory sentencing law. This best solution is difficult, of course, because the political sector will have to eat a very large amount of crow to do it.

Although desirable and, indeed, critical, repeal alone provides no inoculation against recurrence of the disease. Mandatory minimum sentencing is often reinvented as a suddenly discovered anticrime panacea. It is quite likely to reemerge no matter how many times it is proven unsuccessful.

Fortunately, a second approach has been developed. Federal law authorizes judges to depart from the Federal Sentencing Guidelines whenever factors are present that were not "adequately taken into consideration by the Sentencing Commission" when preparing the guidelines. This permits courts to take into account any of the purposes of sentencing set forth in 18 U.S.C. §3553(a), including prevention of further crime by the defendant, rehabilitation if possible, and deterrence.

The same approach can be adopted with regard to mandatory sentences. This could most easily be achieved by statutory amendment. But where a particular sentence is egregiously unfair, interpretation of the purpose of the law may also offer a remedy. As stated by Chief Justice Harlan Stone in a constitutional context: "To decide, we turn to the words . . . read in their historical setting as revealing the purposes of [the] framers, and search for admissible meanings of . . . [the] words which, in the circumstances of their application, will effectuate those purposes."

As Alexander Hamilton stated in *The Federalist*:

> [I]t is not with a view to infractions of the Constitution only, that the independence of the judges may be an essential safeguard . . . [against] injury . . . by unjust and partial laws. Here also the firmness of the judicial magistracy is of vast importance *in mitigating the severity and confining the operation* of such laws.

Article III of the Constitution, in creating an independent judiciary, may include Hamilton's conception of its role and thus mandate use of purpose interpretation where called for by the circumstances. When interpretation does not suffice to avoid injustice, the Eighth Amendment's guarantee against cruel and unusual punishment may be invoked.

Relevant Factors

Some of my own decisions departing from the Federal Sentencing Guidelines may illustrate the kinds of factors that may be relevant to departure from mandatory minimums as well, whether permitted by statutory amendment, purpose interpretation, or adherence to the Constitution:

• Instances in which a family or close-knit religious or other community will provide detailed backup for supervision of a good candidate for rehabilitation, when the guideline sentence was necessary as a deterrent to others.

• Cases where "boot camp" may offer a combination of punishment and rehabilitation that is better for society than long-term imprisonment.

• Instances where a sentence would otherwise be ratcheted to a higher level because of prior events not of a heinous nature and not taken seriously in the geographic area where they occurred.

• Cases in which a small-time operation not posing a significant threat to the public was involved and the prosecution arguably was brought chiefly for statistical reasons.

• Situations in which arrest and conviction decisively prevent further crime of the only type a defendant is likely to commit, but not those where merely one means has been eliminated.

• Situations in which upward departures are important to protect the public from further criminal activity—especially involving violence or threats of violence, large-scale activity, or retention of ill-gotten gains.

For appropriate departures to be encouraged where indicated, sentences should be considered not an ordinary question of law but a matter subject to review only for abuse of discretion. Appellate review could be limited to instances where the appellate court grants leave—akin to a grant of a petition for certiorari [a writ of a superior court to call up the records of an inferior court]—because of reason to believe that a particular sentence was substantially excessive or inadequate.

Hidden Benefits

According to an aphorism attributed to Walt Whitman, some evils have value because of the disputes they cause. That cannot be said of mandatory minimum sentencing because of the human tragedy wreaked by this bulldozing of people that results from looking only at the statutory description of a crime and not at any mitigating factors in deciding how a defendant should be treated.

Despite the massive tragedy continuing to unfold, some benefit can be derived if the public begins to recognize that panaceas are often counterproductive. People may learn that the judiciary should not be robotized and that even entrenched errors can be corrected. Moreover, the justified anger at criminal behavior that is now siphoned into ill-considered pressure for mandatory minimum sentences can be rechanneled into more productive efforts to deal with both the real weaknesses of law enforcement and the factors tending to promote crime.

"Minimum sentences are perhaps the single most important law enforcement tool available to prosecutors in targeting and successfully convicting high-level drug dealers."

MANDATORY MINIMUM SENTENCING IS NECESSARY

Jay Apperson

Jay Apperson argues in the following viewpoint that mandatory minimum sentences work. According to Apperson, mandatory minimum sentences are a powerful, effective weapon against high-level drug traffickers; the threat of swift and lengthy punishment motivates low-level drug users, who wish to reduce their own sentence, to cooperate with the government by identifying their drug source and providing other valuable information. The end result, Apperson claims, is a chain of successful convictions of major drug dealers who inflict massive damage on society and who might otherwise walk free. Apperson is a federal prosecutor in Virginia.

As you read, consider the following questions:

1. According to Apperson, why were couriers and mules often willing to serve jail or prison time before the enactment of mandatory minimums?
2. Why does the author believe that mandatory minimums did not unfairly target Derrick Curry?
3. Why is Apperson not concerned about those defendants who cannot provide information that would reduce their sentence?

Reprinted from Jay Apperson, "Why Prosecutors Back Minimum Sentencing," *Washington Post National Weekly Edition*, March 7–13, 1994, by permission of the author.

Former Deputy Attorney General Philip Heymann has drawn favorable editorial comment . . . for his criticism of mandatory minimum sentences for drug-related and other serious federal crimes. Yet most front-line federal prosecutors including those who deal with narcotics and organized crime cases strongly support tough mandatory minimum sentences for drug trafficking.

Had Heymann asked us, we would have told him why: Minimum sentences are perhaps the single most important law enforcement tool available to prosecutors in targeting and successfully convicting high-level drug dealers. Moreover, the minimums are not absolute: Low-level defendants can avoid them by cooperating with prosecutors.

Real cases, tried by real prosecutors with real results, provide the best evidence. Let me tell you about one of them, a case I tried in the Eastern District of Virginia in 1988, *United States v. Angela Lewis & "Sincere" Ernest.*

LAWS THAT WORK

When I first saw Angela Lewis, she was standing before a federal magistrate, charged with drug trafficking. She was petrified by the experience, terrified about what she was going to tell her family. She was 19 and a successful student with a future. She had never been in trouble with the law. She did not use drugs. She was a perfect example of the people that critics say are punished unfairly by mandatory minimums. And she was also a perfect example of the people the mandatory minimum sentencing scheme is designed to help.

Charged with Angela Lewis was one "Sincere" Ernest, sometime rap singer, part-time boyfriend, full-time crack dealer. He did not use drugs. He used people. Lewis later testified that Ernest bragged to her about his thriving business and told her that he had a lot of people selling drugs for him in Washington, D.C., because the people there were "so stupid" that they'd waste their money on dope.

Ernest and Angela flew to New York together before Memorial Day 1988. On the way back, he stuffed a paper bag in her jacket and told her to wear it on the plane to Washington, making her his "mule." According to Angela, she told him, "If that's drugs, I don't want to carry them." Ernest told her that if she didn't wear the jacket, she wouldn't get back to Washington. He sat apart from her on the plane, and waited for her to catch up with him at National Airport. They were both arrested at the terminal. But it was Angela who was carrying the drugs.

On the way to jail, Angela later said, Ernest asked her to "take the rap" for him, and since she had no criminal record, she'd only do "short time"—call it, Drug Sentence Lite.

We tried to get her to cooperate, and turn evidence on Ernest. But she wouldn't. Without her help, we had to drop the charges against him. But with so much evidence against her, we easily convicted Angela. Mandatory minimums required that she get at least 10 years (the 300 grams of crack she was carrying was six times the 50-gram amount that triggers the mandatory minimum).

The sentencing judge disregarded the statute and sentenced Lewis to six months. He expressed the sympathetic view motivating many current critics: "(She's) 19 years old, a good student and has no record of crime or drug involvement."

I successfully appealed the judge's sentence, and after almost two years of briefs and arguments to the appellate court, the judge was ordered to resentence Lewis to 10 years. Guess what? Within 24 hours of that sentence, I heard from Lewis and her attorney. Lewis, it seems, wasn't ready to do 10 years for Ernest. She was ready to cooperate. With her help, we arrested Ernest, who was convicted and is serving 21 years in federal prison.

The tragedy is that during the almost two years it took to reverse the sentence, Ernest had been running a crack house in the Tidewater area and laundering drug profits into rap music albums starring—yep—"Sincere" Ernest. During that time I have no doubt that other Angela Lewises were recruited, used and discarded by Ernest, other victims preyed upon and more poison distributed. This would not have happened if the system had been allowed to work as intended.

A POWERFUL INCENTIVE

The opponents of mandatory minimums paint a picture of federal prosecutors rounding up unfortunate drug addicts and low-level mules, tossing them into jail for 10 years and moving on to the next case. The reality is quite different.

Unlike state drug cases, federal prosecutions attempt to focus on long-term conspiracies involving increasingly sophisticated and violent international operations. Our experience is that without tough mandatory minimum sentences, defendants facing a few years time are generally willing to serve it, rather than finger violent suppliers and big-time traffickers.

Mandatory minimums are part of a comprehensive scheme that includes the government's ability to reduce a defendant's sentence below the mandatory when the defendant provides "substantial assistance" in the prosecution of others. Assistant U.S. attorneys have, by and large, insisted that substantial assistance means moving "up the ladder" to convict higher-up suppliers—those who run the operations. These thugs deliberately insulate themselves from directly dealing drugs. They use little people like Angela Lewis to do the dirty work and take the rap.

Before mandatory minimums, the underlings (couriers and mules) served little jail time for the scutwork. They were often paid for their prison time by their bosses; their short sentences were simply the cost of doing business. Needless to say, they didn't turn in those bosses. However, faced with the certainty of a 10-year mandatory with no parole, it's amazing how a defendant's fear or "loyalty" is suddenly put into perspective. The defendants suddenly realize they will be giving up a huge chunk of their lives for someone else, who walks away scot free.

KEEPING CRIMINALS OFF THE STREET

Combating violent crime is largely a matter of arresting and incarcerating a relatively small group of predators, many of whom commit more than a hundred crimes a year.

University of Pennsylvania criminologist Marvin Wolfgang studied the Philadelphia arrest records of males born there in 1945 and in 1958. He found that 7 percent of each group committed two-thirds of all violent crime.

Does anyone doubt that the same situation exists in every American city? I do not. Clearly, protecting our families and communities from crime means keeping these thugs off the streets.

A promising start was made during the 1980s when Congress enacted mandatory minimum prison sentences after discovering that defendants with serious criminal records often received very gentle treatment from judges, which was then further softened by parole boards.

By establishing a floor beneath which federal judges could not descend in imposing sentences for certain crimes, such as drug trafficking near schools, and by eliminating the possibility of parole from federal prisons, Congress made sure that hardened criminals would be rendered harmless for substantial periods.

Phil Gramm, *Washington Times*, October 10, 1993.

Those arrested in federal drug cases are told immediately that they face tough mandatory minimums and that their only way out is to cooperate with the government, identify their sources, work in conjunction with undercover agents and testify in court.

One person who was given that chance was Derrick Curry. A writer for the *Washington Post* lamented Curry's "incomprehensibly severe" 20-year sentence for this "small-time dealer." The article didn't report the full range of Curry's known drug dealings as revealed by FBI incident reports, surveillance logs and supporting affidavits and testimony at Curry's trial: Curry had, for example, distributed crack to the undercover agent two previous times; the half kilo of crack recovered from his station wagon was in addition to another full kilo he had just delivered to a co-conspirator; a 12-gauge shotgun was found in his apartment when he was arrested with his co-conspirator.

Curry, the article did note, steadfastly refused to cooperate by "ratting on his friends." Friends? Are these the same kind of "friends" who gave Maryland basketball player Len Bias the coke that killed him? The same "friends" who supply poison to kids in our neighborhoods? It is not the mandatory minimums that are ruining "an entire generation of young black men," as the article suggested, it is drug dealers such as Curry and their higher-up suppliers.

Curry may be content that his suppliers are continuing to work while he protects them and serves their time for them. But I'm not. And neither are most Americans.

SAFETY MECHANISMS

Here's what is missing from the public debate: Mandatory minimum mechanisms were designed to help people exactly like Derrick Curry and Angela Lewis dig themselves out of the holes they had crawled into. They were designed to help Curry and to hurt his suppliers and bosses, who use people like Kleenex and throw them away when they're done.

If Curry wants to help these ringleaders stay out of jail, he can stay in jail. He could have chosen to work with the system. He chose not to.

Fortunately, most defendants, like Lewis, make a different choice. These result in convictions in case after case of higher-level traffickers who would otherwise escape prosecution.

PREVENTING INJUSTICE

There is, to be sure, a small fraction of defendants who are unable to provide the assistance that would reduce their sentences. In my experience, this number is minuscule. But beyond that, Attorney General Janet Reno has provided line prosecutors with additional flexibility in charging decisions to prevent an injustice in those cases where a defendant truly cannot provide information. Her action provides for flexibility without gutting the effectiveness of the mandatory minimums. Congress and the administration should resist current efforts to undercut mandatory minimums legislatively. At the very least, the public needs to know that mandatory minimums work.

By the way, I moved to have Angela Lewis's sentence reduced because of her "substantial assistance" to the United States. Far from languishing in prison, she was free after only 18 months. She now lives with her daughter and is enrolled in a community college. She is staying away from drugs, and those who run them.

"Keeping violent criminals
incarcerated for at least 85 percent
of their sentences would be the
quickest, surest route to safer streets,
schools, and homes."

STATES SHOULD ADOPT TRUTH-IN-SENTENCING LAWS

James Wootton

Americans are suffering a serious epidemic of violent crime, according to James Wootton. In the following viewpoint, Wootton urges state and federal officials to increase public safety by enacting truth-in-sentencing laws, which would require violent criminals to serve at least 85 percent of their sentences. Wootton argues that early-release prisoners—who elude incarceration through probation or parole—are out in the public committing new offenses, causing crime rates to skyrocket. The expense of keeping these offenders behind bars, Wootton contends, is small in relation to the cost of crimes that would be prevented by truth-in-sentencing legislation, including intangible costs to the victims. Wootton is founder and president of the Safe Streets Alliance in Washington, D.C., and is the author of the Chapman truth-in-sentencing amendment to the 1994 federal crime bill.

As you read, consider the following questions:

1. According to the author, how many Americans are likely to be victims of violent crime?
2. In the author's opinion, why is it inappropriate to release convicted criminals on parole?
3. According to Wootton, would truth-in-sentencing laws have a deterrent effect? Why or why not?

Reprinted from James Wootton, "Truth in Sentencing: Why States Should Make Violent Criminals Do Their Time," *State Backgrounder*, December 1993, by permission of the Heritage Foundation.

Not surprisingly, Americans are increasingly alarmed at news stories of violent crimes committed by individuals who had received long sentences for other crimes and yet were released after serving only a small fraction of their time. This alarm is legitimate, because a high proportion of such early-release prisoners commit serious crimes after being released. If crime is to be reduced in America, this trend needs to be reversed. Experience shows clearly that the first step in fighting crime is to keep violent criminals off the street. Keeping violent criminals incarcerated for at least 85 percent of their sentences would be the quickest, surest route to safer streets, schools, and homes.

Government statistics on release practices in 36 states and the District of Columbia in 1988 show that although violent offenders received an average sentence of seven years and eleven months imprisonment, they actually served an average of only two years and eleven months in prison—or only 37 percent of their imposed sentences. The statistics also show that, typically, 51 percent of violent criminals were discharged from prison in two years or less, and 76 percent were back on the streets in four years or less.

Consider the median sentence and time served in prison for those released for the first time in 1988:

COMPARING SENTENCES AND TIME SERVED

Offense	Median Sentence	Median Time Served
Murder	15 years	5.5 years
Rape	8 years	3 years
Robbery	6 years	2.25 years
Assault	4 years	1.25 years

Source: Bureau of Justice Statistics, U.S. Department of Justice

James Wootton, *State Backgrounder*, December 1993.

When these prisoners are released early, a high percentage commit more violent crimes. A three-year follow up of 108,850 state prisoners released in 1983 from institutions in eleven states found that within three years 60 percent of violent offenders were rearrested for a felony or serious misdemeanor, 42 percent were reconvicted, and 37 percent were reincarcerated. Of the violent offenders, 35 percent were rearrested for a new violent crime. Among nonviolent prisoners released, 19 percent were rearrested within three years for a new violent crime.

As a result of these lenient early-release practices and the high percentage of crimes committed by criminals released early, Americans are suffering a fearful epidemic of violent crime. Studies indicate that over 25 percent of all males admitted to prison were being reincarcerated after a new trial for a new offense before the prison term for the first offense had expired. Since 1960, the compounding effect of these crimes by prisoners or early-release prisoners has driven the violent crime rate up by over 500 percent. Now eight out of ten Americans are likely to be victims of violent crime at least once in their lives, at a total cost of $140 billion.

Not surprisingly, the fear of violent crime is intensifying. Polls indicate a growing loss of public confidence in their personal safety and the safety of their streets and neighborhoods. Some 90 percent of Americans think the crime problem is growing, and 43 percent say there is more crime in their neighborhood than there was a year ago. The reason: despite rising arrest rates and prison overcrowding, 3.2 million convicted felons are out on parole or probation rather than in prison. . . .

HIGH RECIDIVISM: THE FAILURE OF PAROLE

Releasing violent criminals from prison before they have completed their sentences is justified by proponents for one of three reasons: first, prisons are overcrowded and it is too costly to build more prisons; second, "good time" credits, which have the effect of reducing sentences, are and should be given to well-behaved prisoners; and third, prisoners sometimes can be rehabilitated, and so should be paroled.

The problem is that the evidence seriously questions the second and third rationales, and shows the first to be very short-sighted.

Recidivism among violent criminals is high. Consider a three-year follow-up of 108,850 state prisoners released in 1983 from institutions in eleven states, conducted by the Bureau of Justice Statistics. The study, the conclusions of which are consistent with those of other such studies, found that within three years some 60 percent of violent offenders were rearrested for a felony or serious misdemeanor; 42 percent of all violent offenders released were reincarcerated. Of all the violent offenders released, 36 percent were rearrested for a violent crime. Among nonviolent prisoners released, 19 percent were rearrested within three years for a violent crime.

The prisoners in the study accounted for over 1.6 million arrest charges for the time before they had entered prison and for the three years afterwards. These included nearly 215,000 arrests for violent crimes before going to prison and 50,000 violent crimes within three years after release. Altogether they were arrested for:

- 14,467 homicides
- 7,073 kidnappings
- 23,174 rapes or sexual assaults
- 101,226 robberies
- 107,130 assaults

THE PROBLEMS OF DETERMINING PAROLE

The U.S. Parole Board uses a sophisticated Salient Factor Score (SFS) to guide it in deciding who will be paroled. Unfortunately for law-abiding Americans, the Parole Board turns out to be over-optimistic. Of those classified by the Parole Board staff as "good risks" for parole, the Parole Board assumes that 18 percent will be rearrested and again sentenced to prison for over one year within five years of release. In addition, the Parole Board expects that 29 percent of "fair risks" who are paroled will be resentenced to over a year in prison within five years of release.

Considering the government's—and the American people's—anxiety about risk, this parole policy is remarkable. Where else would such a high failure rate be tolerated, when it results in the death, rape, or injury of ordinary Americans? The Federal Aviation Administration certainly does not allow airplanes to fly with critical parts that fail 29 percent of the time. And the Food and Drug Administration does not allow drugs on the market that have dangerous side effects 18 percent of the time.

Twenty years ago, James Q. Wilson, then a professor of government at Harvard University, asked a basic question about rehabilitation:

> If rehabilitation is the object, and if there is little or no evidence that available correctional systems will produce much rehabilitation, why should any offender be sent to any institution? But to turn them free on the grounds that society does not know how to make them better is to fail to protect society from those crimes they may commit again and to violate society's moral concern for criminality and thus to undermine society's conception of what constitutes proper conduct. [Because the correctional system had not reduced recidivism,] we would view the correctional system as having a very different function—namely, to isolate and to punish. It is a measure of our confusion that such a statement will strike many enlightened readers today as cruel, even barbaric. It is not. It is merely a recognition that society at a minimum must be able to protect itself from dangerous offenders and to impose some costs (other than the stigma and

inconvenience of an arrest and court appearance) on criminal acts; it is also a frank admission that society really does not know how to do much else.

Until there are dramatic improvements in the techniques of rehabilitation and identifying those who can safely be paroled, state legislators would be wise to follow Professor Wilson's admonition: society must protect itself from dangerous offenders and impose real costs on criminal acts. Or, as Douglas Jeffrey, executive vice president of the Claremont Institute, says, "We need to put justice back into the criminal justice system by putting convicted criminals behind bars and keeping them there for appropriate periods of time." If state legislators were to adopt that simple mission, today's unacceptable risks to law-abiding Americans would be reduced.

INCARCERATION SAVES MONEY

While full sentences may mean more spending on prison, lawmakers and taxpayers need to understand that early-release programs cost dollars rather than save them. A 1982 Rand Corporation study of prison inmates found that the average inmate had committed 187 crimes the year before being incarcerated. When criminals are released early, many commit a similar volume of crimes when back on the streets.

The cost of crime committed by these early-release criminals is both direct and indirect. Taxpayers must finance the criminal justice system. Householders and businesses must buy private protection such as lighting, locks, dogs, fences, and alarm systems. They must buy insurance. The victims lose property and wages, and often incur heavy hospitalization costs.

In addition to the direct costs, there is the hidden cost of crime. Businesses, for instance, pass on to customers some of their costs for security and stolen merchandise. Households also must "pay" for crime by altering their behavior and life style. William Greer has estimated that crime increases in the early 1980s caused "150,000 more New Yorkers to take taxis instead of public transportation; some 140,000 more New York City households sacrificed trips rather than leave their apartments unprotected. 50,000 put bars on their windows and 40,000 bought weapons. Even more difficult to assess are the costs of 'urban blight' such as abandoned buildings, unsafe schools, and inner city unemployment. Quite possibly the costs we can't count exceed the ones we can."

It is easy for policy makers to underestimate the tremendous cost of crime, particularly the cost of injuries and deaths of victims. Mark Cohen, a researcher at the U.S. Sentencing Commission, broke new ground in this area in 1988 by using jury verdicts in personal injury cases to estimate the value of injuries to victims. The cost to society of each rape is $51,058, each robbery $12,594, each assault $12,028. These as costs are invisible to all but the victims who are randomly burdened by society's failure to keep repeat offenders in prison.

In 1990, David Cavanagh and Mark Kleiman of the BOTEC Analysis Corporation, a Cambridge, Massachusetts, consulting firm, performed an even more ambitious and complex cost-benefit analysis of incarceration. The analysis includes as many indirect societal costs and benefits as possible. Cavanagh and Kleiman estimate the most plausible range of the cost of incarceration of one inmate per year at $34,000 to $38,000. But the total benefits occurring from incarcerating that one inmate for a year, eliminating the cost of the individual's probable crimes, could run between $172,000 and $2,364,000. In a later paper Cavanagh and Kleiman computed a range of ratios from 3 to 1 to as high as 17 to 1 of benefits over costs. Edward W. Zedlewski, of the National Institute of Justice, estimated a benefit/cost ratio for incarcerating prisoners of 17 to 1.

The 1982 Rand Corporation study finds that the average robber commits between 41 and 61 robberies a year. Mark Cohen estimates that the actual cost to society of each robbery is $12,569. Assuming the cost to society of keeping a robber in prison is Cavanagh and Kleiman's high estimate of $37,614 a year; from a strictly financial point of view it makes sense to incarcerate a robber if that individual commits three or more robberies each year.

INVESTING IN SAFETY

The imprisonment rate is higher in the United States than it is in other Western democracies mainly because Americans commit crime at a higher rate. The homicide rate in the United States is five times as high as in Europe; the rape rate is more than six times as high; and the robbery rate is four times as high.

Given the higher crime rates in the United States, and the benefits to society of incarcerating criminals, state and federal officials have underinvested in public safety. According to one estimate, more than 120,000 additional prison beds were needed across the nation at the close of 1990. Some might argue that some inmates do not belong in prison, and should be replaced with hardened criminals. But 95 percent of Americans in prison are repeat or violent offenders. Despite this enormous need for additional prison space, spending on corrections remains a very small percentage of state and local budgets. In fiscal year 1990, only 2.5 percent of the $975.9 billion in total expenditures by state and local governments went for corrections (about $24.7 billion). Investment in new prison construction is only a small fraction of that figure. . . .

WHY TRUTH IN SENTENCING HELPS

Truth in sentencing will increase the length of time convicted violent criminals are incarcerated. Currently violent criminals are serving 37 percent of the sentence that has been imposed. If required to serve at least 85 percent of their sentences, violent criminals would serve 2.3 times longer than they do now.

If the 55 percent of the estimated 800,000 current state and federal prisoners who are violent offenders were subject to serving 85 percent of their sentence, and assuming that those violent offenders would have committed ten violent crimes a year while on the street, then the number of crimes prevented each year by truth in sentencing would be 4,400,000. That would be over two-thirds of the 6,000,000 violent crimes reported in the National Criminal Victims Survey for 1990.

TARGETING HARDENED CRIMINALS

Truth-in-sentencing laws would require state prison officials to retain more prisoners, at a higher cost to the state. But research shows that these prisoners are generally society's most dangerous predators. In a landmark study, University of Pennsylvania criminologist Marvin Wolfgang compiled arrest records up to their 30th birthday for every male born and raised in Philadelphia in 1945 and 1958. He found that just 7 percent of each age group committed two-thirds of all violent crime, including three-fourths of the rapes and robberies and virtually all of the murders. Moreover, this 7 percent not only had five or more arrests by age 18 but went on committing felonies. Wolfgang and his colleagues estimate these criminals got away with about a dozen crimes. Their studies suggest that about 75,000 new, young, persistent criminal predators are added to the population every year. They hit their peak rate of offenses at about age 16.

In response to these findings, Alfred Regnery, who was Administrator of the Office of Juvenile Justice and Delinquency Prevention at the Justice Department from 1982 to 1986, funded projects in cities in which police, prosecutors, schools, and welfare and probation workers pooled information to focus on the "serious habitual offender." The program had a significant effect in many cities. Thanks to this Justice Department program, for example, Oxnard, California, was able to place the city's thirty most active serious habitual offenders behind bars, and violent crimes dropped 38 percent in 1987, more than double the drop in any other California city. By 1989, when all thirty of the active serious habitual offenders were behind bars, murders declined 60 percent compared with 1980, robberies 41 percent and burglaries 29 percent.

Thus in conjunction with a criminal justice system that convicts and incarcerates the hardened criminals, a truth-in-sentencing policy will reduce crime by keeping these serious and habitual offenders in prison longer.

HOW TRUTH-IN-SENTENCING DETERS CRIMINALS

Incarceration incapacitates violent criminals, and directly benefits law-abiding Americans, by protecting families and also by yielding greater financial savings from reduced crime than the cost of incarceration itself. But stepped-up imprisonment also deters crime. Criminologist Isaac Ehrlich of the University of Chicago estimated that a one percent increase in arrest rates produces a one point decrease in crime rates, and a one percent increase in sentence length produces a one percent decrease in crime rates, for a combined deterrent and incapacitation effect of 1.1 percent. Observed trends seem to support Ehrlich's broad conclusion and hence the claim of deterrence. When the rate of imprisonment per 100 crimes began dropping in the early 1960s, for instance, the rate of crime per 100 population began to climb steeply.

A recent report by the Dallas-based National Center for Policy Analysis, written by Texas A&M economist Morgan Reynolds, makes a strong case for the deterrence value of longer sentences. According to Reynolds:

> Crime has increased as the expected costs of committing crimes has fallen. Today, for a burglary, for example, the chance of arrest is 7 percent. If you are unlucky enough to be one of the 7 percent arrested, relax; only 87 percent of arrestees are prosecuted. Of those, only 79 percent are convicted. Then only 25 percent of those convicted actually go to prison. Multiplying out all these probabilities gives your would-be burglar a 1.2 percent chance of going to jail.

So, too many criminals do not go to jail for the crimes they commit. Reynolds points out that "once in prison, a burglar will stay there for about 13 months, but since more than 98 percent of burglaries never result in a prison sentence, the average expected sentence for each act of burglary is only 4.8 days. Similar calculations yield an expected punishment in 1990 of 1.8 years for murder, 60.5 days for rape, and 6.7 days for arson. Thus, for every crime, the expected punishment has declined over the decades. The decline continues between 1988 and 1990. When punishments rise, crime falls." In short, Reynolds's argument is that raising expected punishment deters crime. Expected punishment is a function of the risk of being caught and convicted multiplied by the median time served. Therefore, everything being equal, increasing the length of sentence increases expected punishment, and hence a criminal is more likely to be deterred when the sentence is longer.

Reynolds also finds that since 1960, the expected punishment for committing a serious crime in Texas has dropped by more than two-thirds, while the number of serious crimes per 100,000 population in Texas has increased more than sixfold.

While these data do not separate out the deterrent effect of longer sentences from the incapacitation effect, it is clear that longer sentences can generally be expected to reduce crime rates.

OBJECTIONS TO TRUTH-IN-SENTENCING LAWS

State truth-in-sentencing laws have great potential to combat violent crime. While academics and legislators in Washington and the states often focus on long-term solutions to the crime problem, such as social or economic conditions or the "root causes" of crime, the special merit of the truth-in-sentencing approach is simply that it keeps violent criminals off the streets while citizens, legislators, and professionals debate the merits of differing approaches in relative safety. In spite of its appeal to common sense, opponents of truth-in-sentencing legislation often make invalid objections. Some argue that truth in sentencing simply costs too much. But such an objection overlooks the opportunity cost of not keeping dangerous offenders in prison. For example, the cost of incarcerating a criminal is approximately $23,000 per year, but the cost of that criminal on the street is $452,000 per year. Some financial estimates are much higher. And, of course, for the families and victims of violent crime, such as James Jordan and Polly Klaas, the human cost is beyond calculation. Others argue that the already large numbers of persons in American jails is an international scandal. While there are indeed more criminals in America who serve more time than criminals in other countries, the fact remains that the violent crime rate in America is proportionately higher than in virtually all other countries. And if there is any scandal, it is the perpetuation of a failing criminal justice system that allows convicted rapists, kidnappers, and armed robbers back on the streets, ignoring the concerns of an American public that desperately needs security from predatory, violent criminals.

Beyond the questions of cost and the higher percentage of individuals being incarcerated, another objection to the enactment of truth-in-sentencing laws is that they ignore the "root causes" of crime. These root causes are often discussed in terms of persistent poverty, poor education, and deteriorating families. Liberal academics, of course, are not alone in addressing these maladies; and conservative social criticism, including recent analyses by scholars from the Heritage Foundation, have enriched the growing national debate on America's failing criminal justice system. But an academic focus on "root causes," whatever its long-term impact on public policy, should not ignore the fact that violent crime itself immediately aggravates these social problems. . . .

The time has come for states to enact truth-in-sentencing laws. There are few viable alternatives that protect citizens from the immediate threat of violent crime. Parole, for example, is a failed experiment. The American people deserve better.

| "'Truth in sentencing' may be one of the most misunderstood concepts in the criminal justice field."

STATES SHOULD NOT ADOPT TRUTH-IN-SENTENCING LAWS

Marc Mauer

In the following viewpoint, Marc Mauer argues that truth-in-sentencing laws are more complex than they appear, and therefore policy makers must examine the usefulness and consequences of such policies before enacting legislation. While restoring "truth" to the sentencing process is touted as a powerful weapon against criminal behavior, Mauer contends that these policies have potential drawbacks, including the massive costs of increasing incarceration with only a dubious impact on crime control. Mauer maintains that public dissatisfaction with early-release policies is not legitimate because judges and attorneys usually tailor sentences according to prison release policies. He also notes that truth in sentencing may not be evenly applied due to variations in state sentencing policies. Mauer is the assistant director of the Sentencing Project in Washington, D.C.

As you read, consider the following questions:

1. According to the author, how might truth in sentencing actually result in more lenient sentences?
2. According to Mauer, what problems do parole boards face?
3. How does the author refute James Wootton's suggestion that truth-in-sentencing legislation could cut violent crime by more than two-thirds?

Reprinted from Marc Mauer, "The Truth About Truth in Sentencing," Corrections Today, February 1996.

"Truth in sentencing" may be one of the most misunderstood concepts in the criminal justice field. At a time when policymakers at the state and national level are promoting various truth-in-sentencing schemes, it is important to examine the broad range of goals, objectives and ideologies that are tied to this concept.

In recent years, truth in sentencing has gained much prominence at the federal level. The federal sentencing guidelines that went into effect in 1987 incorporated truth in sentencing, whereby offenders are required to serve at least 85 percent of their sentence. Both the 1994 and 1995 federal crime bills contained provisions to encourage states to adopt truth in sentencing as a condition of receiving federal prison construction aid. States that require that violent offenders serve at least 85 percent of their sentences are eligible for funding from the truth-in-sentencing portion of the $10 billion package of federal assistance.

A number of states also have adopted varying types of truth-in-sentencing legislation in recent years. These have been developed in a variety of ways—as part of efforts to abolish parole, to adopt certain kinds of determinate sentencing guidelines and to implement other sentencing reforms.

Clearly, the impact of truth in sentencing will vary tremendously depending on the type of policy adopted and the goals behind it. In order to assess its impact, we need to understand the rationales and goals of these various policies.

As this assessment is done, what becomes even more clear is the need to examine both the intended and unintended consequences of such policies, such as what impact these policies will have on public safety, prison populations and the cost of corrections. Policies such as these also raise fundamental questions about decision-making within the criminal justice system—that is, to what extent it is desirable to maintain discretion within the system and, if so, in which parts of the system that discretion should reside. Once we begin to address these questions, we find that the development of effective and rational policy is more complex than it might appear at first.

GOALS OF TRUTH IN SENTENCING

Before we can assess the usefulness and impact of truth-in-sentencing policies, it is necessary to define the various goals of these policies. These generally can be categorized under three sometimes overlapping areas:

- To restore "truth" in the sentencing process so the public knows how much time an offender will serve in prison.

- To increase the proportion of a sentence that is served in prison, generally to 85 percent, and/or to eliminate parole release as a means of reducing crime by keeping offenders incarcerated for a longer period of time.
- To control the use of prison space, often in conjunction with a guidelines system, so decision makers know in advance what the impact of sentencing will be on prison populations

TRUTH IN SENTENCING'S IMPACT

An assessment of the potential impact of truth-in-sentencing policies requires first that we define the various policies that fall under this terminology and second, that we consider their stated goals.

Restoring "truth" to the sentencing process. An argument frequently made by proponents of truth in sentencing is that the public is confused and deceived about how much time offenders will serve in prison. For example, in an indeterminate sentencing state a burglar might receive a sentence of three to five years but be released on parole after serving "only" two years.

The source of this public dissatisfaction goes beyond just the perceived "untruthfulness" of the sentencing process. At a basic level, it reflects the general public fear of crime. Crime rates rose significantly in the 1960s and '70s, and the public's fear of crime began to escalate as well. People's fear of victimization, whether accurate or not, often focuses on the criminal justice system as the source of their problems, since common sense suggests that the system should be able to "cure" crime.

The criminal justice system further aggravates these feelings with a confusing array of charging, sentencing and parole procedures that generally are understood only by the lawyers, judges and administrators who employ them. So, average Americans who are not familiar with the intricacies of parole and good time statutes and the beneficial role they play become angry when they learn that a particularly notorious offender was released from prison after serving "only" half his sentence, for example.

One irony of this situation is that for the vast majority of cases in the court system, the public usually has little or no information and is completely unaware of either sentencing statutes or practices. It is only in an unusual case, generally one in which a heinous crime has been committed by an offender who is perceived to have been released early, that public anger surfaces. Whether these cases are at all typical or understandable is rarely discussed.

Are these perceptions legitimate? Is the court system being untruthful? Not really. While the public may not be aware of the intricacies of sentencing policy, there is little misunderstanding in the courtroom when a prison sentence is pronounced. Judges generally are quite aware of prison release policies and often will tailor their sentences accordingly. If a judge feels that an offender should spend two years in prison, he or she will sentence the offender to a three-year term if current parole policies generally result in inmates being released after serving two-thirds of their sentence. Likewise, the prosecutor, defense attorney and, generally, the defendant all have a good working knowledge of sentencing and release practices. . . .

INDETERMINATE SENTENCING

Much of the source of concern about incorporating truth in the sentencing process stems from misunderstandings about the indeterminate sentencing system, which was the dominant form of sentencing nationally for many years and still prevails in many states today. Under indeterminate sentencing, a judge sets a maximum term of imprisonment and an administrative agency, the parole board, determines how much of the term the offender will actually serve.

In most states, a prisoner is eligible to be considered for parole release after serving a fixed percentage of the minimum sentence, often half or two-thirds. Historically, these systems were established to provide incentives for good behavior in prison and to encourage inmates to make progress toward parole release plans. Release on parole was not considered to be an early release, but rather a rational decision concerning the appropriate time at which an offender could be released to the community with minimal risk.

The problem with any type of sentencing or release decision-making system, of course, is that human judgments are not infallible and mistakes are, and always will be, made. In addition, the dramatic rise in the prison population in recent years has created enormous workloads for parole boards. In most states today, a parole board is only able to meet with a prisoner for a few minutes and in some states only a review of records is possible.

Due to public dissatisfaction and misunderstanding of the sentencing and parole processes, a movement emerged to restore truth to the sentencing process. What exactly this means is not always clear. Albert Alschuler has remarked, for example, that if we were concerned only with truth at the time of sentencing, then the "judge should have been required to announce this [release] date through a bullhorn" so that the public would be well informed. . . .

The idea that truth should be inserted into the sentencing decision unfortunately overlooks other aspects of the system in which the court process or terminology does not always correspond with the crime committed or the punishment imposed. Most significantly, the plea bargaining process, which is essential to the functioning of the court system, often results in convictions that have little relationship to the crime that was committed.

STATE SENTENCING POLICIES

Another limitation of truth in sentencing pertains to overall state sentencing policies. Truth in sentencing and state sentencing policies are two different practices. Truth in sentencing, for example, tells us how long an offender will spend in prison. State sentencing policy, on the other hand, dictates what types of crimes will result in prison or jail sentences, probation or some alternative. Sentencing policies, not truth in sentencing, indicate which offenders (violent as opposed to property, for example) will be incarcerated.

While truth in sentencing implies harsher sentencing policies, in practice this may not be the case. In Louisiana, for example, Secretary of Public Safety and Corrections Richard Stalder has reported that inmates serve about 50 percent of their prison terms on average. Yet, because prison sentences are quite harsh in that state, the 50 percent of time served generally is longer than the 85 percent of time served in some truth-in-sentencing states. . . .

Increasing time served in prison or eliminating parole release through truth in sentencing. A primary objective of truth-in-sentencing advocates in recent years has been to increase the period of time served in prison; the target often has been violent offenders. States such as Arizona, Missouri and Virginia have passed legislation in recent years to require that violent offenders serve at least 85 percent of their imposed sentence.

Proponents of such truth-in-sentencing laws generally argue that such policies will reduce crime through incapacitation. If the average violent offender currently serves about 48 percent of the imposed sentence, then almost doubling this to 85 percent will reduce potential crimes that these offenders might otherwise commit upon release. James Wootton, director of the Safe Streets Alliance, one of the major organizations behind these proposals, has even suggested that such policies could cut violent crime by more than two-thirds.

A Questionable Impact on Crime

In a 1993 paper on truth in sentencing prepared for the Heritage Foundation, Wootton calculates that truth in sentencing could prevent more than 4 million of the 6 million violent crimes committed each year. He comes to this conclusion by suggesting that if the approximately 440,000 violent offenders incarcerated (in 1992) were required to serve 85 percent of their sentence and that if each would have otherwise committed ten violent crimes a year, then more than 4 million crimes would be prevented.

Are such dramatic declines in violent crime possible through a single piece of legislation? Unfortunately, no. Rather than debate theoretically about whether this would be successful, we can look at real-life evidence regarding this assumption.

Age-Specific Murder Rates (1985 and 1992)

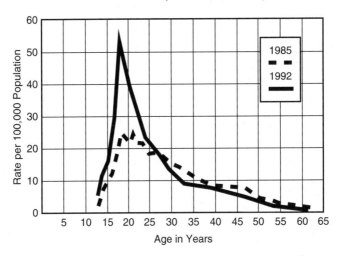

Source: "Age-Specific Arrest Rates and Race-Specific Arrest Rates for Selected Offenses, 1965–1992," Uniform Crime Reporting Program, FBI, Washington, DC: December 1993.

Marc Mauer, *Corrections Today*, February 1996.

Examining only the period 1986–91, the number of violent offenders in state prisons increased from approximately 247,000 to 331,000. By Wootton's calculations, this increase of 84,000 violent offenders should have prevented 840,000 violent crimes, or an overall decline of 15 percent from the 5.5 million violent victimizations in 1986.

What actually happened to violent crime during this time?

Victimization surveys by the Department of Justice show that violent victimizations increased by more than 1 million, or 19 percent, during this period. Wootton's argument for a two-thirds drop in violent crime is clearly not plausible.

Requiring violent offenders to serve 85 percent of their sentence probably would have some impact on crime, but it likely would be a relatively modest impact at great cost. Although common sense would suggest that locking up violent offenders for longer periods of time would seem to be a means of cutting crime, a closer examination of the demographics of crime commission reveals why this impact is so limited.

It is well-known that males in the 15 to 24 age group commit a disproportionate amount of crime, and that rates of crime fall fairly dramatically in the succeeding age cohorts. Wootton's analysis, though, assumes that the group of offenders currently incarcerated would continue committing crimes at a high rate virtually forever, when arrest data show us that this is not the case. Further, the analysis assumes that there is a static group of violent offenders in the population. This ignores the fact that there is a new cohort of 15-year-olds entering the high crime rate years annually. Thus, while some offenders are "aging out" of crime, younger offenders are constantly "replacing" them. Studies of criminal careers also show that violent offenses often are committed in the course of a criminal "career" that is basically nonviolent. The National Research Council, in its comprehensive study "Understanding and Preventing Violence," concluded, "Most recorded violent crimes occur in the course of long, active criminal careers dominated by property offenses." Thus, while incapacitating violent offenders for longer periods of time might prevent some crimes, these crimes are more likely to be property offenses rather than violent offenses. . . .

Truth in sentencing as a means of allocating prison space rationally. The third common way in which truth in sentencing is employed is in conjunction with sentencing policies that attempt to achieve a rational allocation of prison space. Several states, including Kansas, Minnesota, Oregon, North Carolina and Washington, have developed these types of policies in conjunction with presumptive sentencing guidelines. Other states, such as Delaware, have instituted modified guidelines systems and adopted separate truth-in-sentencing legislation.

TRUTH IN SENTENCING IN DELAWARE

The state of Delaware offers an instructive example of how policymakers adopted truth in sentencing as a means of achieving a more rational use of prison space. In 1984, the state had established the Sentencing Accountability Commission with the charge of establishing a guidelines system of sentencing using varying levels of control, supervision and programming. The commission developed a five-level continuum ranging from incarceration to unsupervised probation, which went into effect in 1987.

LEGISLATION IN DELAWARE

Because of prison crowding, a variety of early release mechanisms had been established in Delaware under which inmates could earn early release. Ironically, some inmates sentenced for relatively long prison terms were released earlier than inmates with less severe sentences because they participated in more programs and earned more release credits.

To address this issue of uncertainty in sentence impact, the legislature enacted a truth-in-sentencing law in 1989. The key elements of the legislation are the following:

- All inmates must serve at least 75 percent of their imposed sentence.
- Serious offenders generally will serve more time in prison than lesser offenders.
- Sentence lengths have been adjusted to approximate actual time served prior to the new legislation.

For persons unfamiliar with parole and good time release, truth in sentencing in this context has the appearance of legislating shorter sentences. An analysis by the Delaware Criminal Justice Council showed that while sex offenders were sentenced to an average of 16.6 years prior to the legislation, under truth in sentencing the average sentence would be 10 years. Time served in prison, though, would increase from an average of 5.5 years to 6.6 years. (After the initial introduction of truth in sentencing, time served was somewhat less than the 75 percent mark due to a number of transitional factors. As of 1994, inmates are serving 75 percent of their terms on average.) Similar changes would take place for other serious offenses, with time served for homicide increasing from 7.9 to 10.5 years, and for robbery, from 2 to 2.5 years.

To avoid crowding the prison system, though, the truth-in-sentencing legislation in Delaware resulted in a decrease in time served for burglary and theft offenses. For burglary, time served declined from one year to six months, and for theft, from 10 months to three.

Not all states with sentencing guidelines have truth in sentencing, and among those that do, the portion of the sentence to be served often is not 85 percent. For example, the guidelines for Kansas and Oregon permit inmates to earn up to 20 percent good time, while Minnesota and Washington provide for up to one-third off the sentence.

A final issue is that a jurisdiction can have a guidelines system and truth in sentencing but have no control over the growth of its prison population. The federal sentencing guidelines are a prime example of this, since they were developed without a significant concern for prison capacity. Since the implementation of the guidelines in 1987, along with other sentencing changes, sentenced offenders now serve 85 percent of their time. While sentence lengths for crimes other than drug offenses have decreased, actual time served in prison has increased for all offenses. In 1986, for example, prior to the adoption of the federal guidelines, released prisoners had served an average of 16 months in prison. By 1992, largely reflecting the influence of the guidelines, time served had increased 50 percent to 24 months, on average. By 1994, the combined impact of the guidelines and mandatory sentencing laws had raised the federal prison population to 93,000 from its 1987 level of 48,000.

The crime bill adopted by Congress in 1994 follows this pattern of encouraging states to adopt truth-in-sentencing policies without any regard for prison system capacity. Because of this, it is anticipated that state prison populations will rise significantly in those states that adopt the truth-in-sentencing provisions, costing the states far more in prison operations than they will receive from the crime bills. . . .

A Responsible Policymaker's Guide to Truth in Sentencing

The preceding analysis has demonstrated that truth in sentencing is a concept with many meanings for many people. For policymakers, the key question is whether truth in sentencing can play a constructive role in criminal justice decision making.

For the truth-in-sentencing goal of restoring truth to the sentencing system, the best one can say is that there is no harm in doing so. This type of policy might help inform the public on the rare occasion in which there is outside attention. Realistically, however, it still leaves a system with a confusing array of charging and plea bargaining practices that are essential to the functioning of the system but that often bear little resemblance to the reality of the crime.

Under the second goal of truth in sentencing—lengthening sentences and/or abolishing parole—there appears to be little to be achieved for corrections systems but many potentially serious drawbacks. As we have seen, attempting to control crime by increasing sentence length is a dubious proposition. The crime control benefits of this approach are inherently limited by the demographics of crime commission, whereby newer and younger offenders enter the "high crime rate" pool and replace older offenders who are "aging out" of crime. In addition, there is little to be gained in general deterrence since certainty of punishment—the odds that an offender will be apprehended and convicted—has been found to be more of a deterrent factor than the severity of punishment.

The one area in which truth in sentencing may benefit the corrections system is through a sentencing guidelines system that is based on existing prison capacity. If state policymakers wish to utilize prison space rationally, such a system allows for front-end decision making based on an overall assessment of the use of prison space over time.

Even in this regard, though, it is important to note the value of the role that well-structured discretion should play throughout the criminal justice system. While some kinds of sentencing guidelines systems (those implemented without a parole mechanism) may place constraints on the abuse of judicial discretion, they also reduce the value of appropriate discretion at the back end of the system, the release decision from prison. For example, a judge sentencing a substance abuser to a certain number of years in prison has no way of knowing at the time of sentencing whether the offender will participate in a treatment program while incarcerated and what level of risk he or she will be considered to present after such programming. Such information is critical in determining when and under what circumstances an offender will be released back to the community.

To answer our original question of what is the truth about truth in sentencing, it turns out that there are many truths. In truth in sentencing, as with any other policy option, policymakers first need to decide where it is they want to go before they can figure out how to get there.

PERIODICAL BIBLIOGRAPHY

The following articles have been selected to supplement the diverse views presented in this chapter. Addresses are provided for periodicals not indexed in the *Readers' Guide to Periodical Literature*, the *Alternative Press Index*, the *Social Sciences Index*, or the *Index to Legal Periodicals and Books*.

Lucy Berliner	"Three Strikes and You're Out: Will the Community Be Safer?" *Journal of Interpersonal Violence*, September 1994. Available from Sage Publications, 2455 Teller Road, Thousand Oaks, CA 91320.
Michael Brennan	"A Case for Discretion: Are Mandatory Minimum Sentences Destroying Our Sense of Justice and Compassion?" *Newsweek*, November 13, 1995.
CQ Researcher	"Mandatory Sentencing," May 26, 1995. Available from 1414 22nd St. NW, Washington, DC 20037.
Nick DiSpoldo	"Three-Strikes Laws: Cruel and Unusual?" *Commonweal*, June 14, 1996.
David R. Francis	"Just Proven: Prisons Do Keep Crime Down," *Christian Science Monitor*, January 19, 1996. Available from One Norway St., Boston, MA 02115.
Mark Fritz	"Prison Pros Point Out Cons of Tougher Sentences," *California Prisoner*, Summer 1995.
Daniel Lungren	"Three Cheers for Three Strikes," *Policy Review*, November/December 1996.
Edwin Meese	"Three-Strikes Laws Punish and Protect," *Insight*, May 16, 1994. Available from 3600 New York Ave. NE, Washington, DC 20002.
Progressive	"Crime of the Century," March 1994.
Joseph Sandoval	"Three Strikes Is Good Criminal Justice Policy," *Corrections Today*, July 1996. Available from the American Correctional Assoc., Inc., 4380 Forbes Blvd., Lanham, MD 20706-4322.
Jerome H. Skolnick	"Wild Pitch: 'Three-Strikes, You're Out' and Other Bad Calls on Crime," *American Prospect*, Spring 1994.
Reginald Stuart	"The Sentencing Game," *Emerge*, May 1996. Available from One BET Plaza, 1900 W. Place NE, Washington, DC 20018-1211.
Franklin Zimring	"Tough Crime Laws Are False Promises," *Insight*, May 16, 1994.

CHAPTER 4

HOW DOES THE LEGAL SYSTEM AFFECT CRIMINAL JUSTICE?

CHAPTER PREFACE

In 1995, former football star and public personality O.J. Simpson was acquitted of the double murder of his ex-wife Nicole Brown and her friend Ronald Goldman. Nationally televised and extensively covered in the media, Simpson's trial received more publicity than perhaps any other case in American history.

Throughout the Simpson trial and in the wake of the not guilty verdict, the legal system—and especially the role of defense attorneys—was thrown into the public spotlight. Because the state had amassed seemingly irrefutable evidence against Simpson, many people charge that he was acquitted only because a host of high-paid defense attorneys brazenly employed tactics to obfuscate the truth. To many, the case proved that defense attorneys have no regard for the truth, but rather will advance any theory—no matter how farfetched—in their client's interests. Attorney Floyd Abrams commented: "The Simpson case raises broad questions about just what it is our society asks lawyers to do, and the breathtakingly amoral way in which they do it."

Others dispute the view that Simpson's attorneys hindered justice by distorting the facts or engaging in trickery. According to USC law professor Erwin Chemerinsky, "In so many ways, the Simpson trial is the legal system at its very best. Excellent prosecutors carefully presented a vast array of often sophisticated evidence and excellent defense attorneys subjected it to rigorous cross-examination." Such proponents maintain that defense attorneys' role is to use every legal means to represent a client. By doing this, defense attorneys protect the interests of every individual who is ever charged with a crime.

Most people agree that every person is entitled to a fair trial when charged with a crime. But whether the tactics employed result in the truth or merely a contest that has nothing to do with justice is debated in the following chapter.

| "The reliance we place in our adversarial trial court system to deliver just decisions is a misguided leap of faith."

THE CRIMINAL TRIAL IS TOO ADVERSARIAL

Franklin Strier

Justice is often the casualty in the American courtroom, according to Franklin Strier. In the following viewpoint, Strier argues that the adversarial system of justice is too often dominated by a sense of showmanship—high drama orchestrated by dueling lawyers—rather than with the search for truth. As an example, Strier analyzes tactics used by both the defense and prosecution during the O.J. Simpson case, charging that they are symptomatic of a trial system that rewards lawyers only for playing well and winning. Strier is professor of law at California State University, Dominguez Hills, California. He is the author of *Reconstructing Justice: An Agenda for Trial Reform*.

As you read, consider the following questions:

1. According to the author, why should attorneys refrain from coaching witnesses?
2. Why did the Simpson prosecution begin its case by presenting evidence of spousal abuse, according to Strier?
3. According to the author, why did O.J. Simpson's attorneys change their defense as the trial proceeded?

From Franklin Strier, "Adversarial Justice." This article appeared in the August 1995 issue and is reprinted with permission from the *World & I*, a publication of The Washington Times Corporation, copyright ©1995.

W e take it as axiomatic that our trial courts dispense justice. The very legitimacy of the courts depends on that expectation. Yet the reliance we place in our adversarial trial court system to deliver just decisions is a misguided leap of faith. This is neither a radical nor novel perspective. Consider, for example, this observation by the eminent jurist Karl Llewellyn:

> The adversary trial seems from outside like back-handedness or trickery which approaches a travesty on justice; a dragging, awkward, unreliable machinery at best; at worst, one which is manipulated. In consequence . . . there is not one sole excrescence of trial machinery that will find one sole jot of support from any person in the court except the lawyer.

Several inherent flaws of the adversary trial system support Llewellyn's assessment, but none more forcefully than the system's weakness in exposing the truth. In a trial, justice without truth is serendipitous. Benjamin Disraeli said, "Justice is truth in action." The U.S. Supreme Court has concurred, frequently stating that the central purpose of the trial is the determination of truth. . . . The sobering reality is that our trials, especially jury trials, are decidedly fickle vehicles to the truth. Justice is the casualty.

FIGHT THEORY

Paradoxes and false presumptions suffuse the theories and concepts undergirding our trial system. One such presumption is sometimes referred to as the *fight theory*, which holds that truth is best revealed in the courtroom through the clash of opposing views, rather than through investigation by the judge or other neutral third parties. Adversary theory presumes that the personal motivation of attorneys will generate the most assiduous search for favorable evidence. Essentially, this is the legal version of the "invisible hand" theory: Each party pursuing his or her own self-interest will adduce the most favorable evidence and generate the best arguments, yielding the fairest possible trial and a just result. By the same token, statements of the opposition will be vigorously monitored. Because the parties (rather than the judge) control the proceedings, rigorous cross-examination of adverse testimony is assumed.

The problem with the fight theory is that it is neither logically supportable nor empirically verifiable. Federal judge Jerome Frank, former chairman of the Securities and Exchange Commission (SEC) and an oft-quoted critic of the adversary system, challenged the fight theory. His premise was simple: "The partisanship of the opposing lawyers blocks the uncovering of vital evidence or leads to a presentation of vital testimony in a way that distorts it." He concluded: "To treat a lawsuit as, above all, a fight, surely cannot be the best way to discover facts. Improvement in fact-finding will necessitate some considerable diminution of the martial spirit in litigation."

Other critics disparage the fight theory. Judge Marvin Frankel, a leader in the movement to give truth a greater value in trials, was shocked by the wanton leap of logic necessary to subscribe to the fight theory. After noting that other truth seekers do not use adversary means, he observed:

> We . . . would fear for our lives if physicians, disagreeing about the cause of our chest pains, sought to resolve the issue by our forms of interrogation, badgering, and other forensics. But for the defendant whose life is at stake—and for the public concerned the defendant is a homicidal menace—this is thought to be the perfect form of inquiry. We live, at any rate, as if we believe this.

Commenting on the implausibility of the truth-from-fight assumption, Thurman Arnold wrote in *The Symbols of Government*:

> Bitter partisanship in opposite directions is supposed to bring out the truth. Of course no rational human being would apply such a theory to his own affairs. . . . Mutual exaggeration of opposing claims violate(s) the whole theory of rational, scientific investigation. Yet in spite of this most obvious fact, the ordinary teacher of law will insist (1) that combat makes for clarity, (2) that heated arguments bring out the truth, and (3) that anyone who doesn't believe this is a loose thinker.

Our use of the fight theory results in a paradox: Trial procedure assigns exclusive responsibility for presenting the evidence to those with no legal or professional obligation to seek the truth—the attorneys. Their goal is victory, not enlightenment. Studies show that attorneys often spend more time trying to hide or distort facts than revealing them. In every trial, at least one attorney usually tries to suppress or cloud unfavorable evidence.

A tenet of the adversary system is that each side's attorney will fight as hard as he can. Thus the attorney's duty of "zealous advocacy" is prescribed in the various professional codes that purport to delineate ethical conduct for attorneys. But this makes adversarial excess endemic to the system. And although we expect attorneys to adhere to the rules of evidence and confine their strategies to the ethical boundaries of the rules, they often bend the rules and stretch the strategies.

PRETRIAL ABUSE

Attorney abuses begin before the trial, during the discovery process. Under discovery, a litigant may request of the opposing party any relevant information (not protected by privilege) which that party has or to which that party has access. One objective was to do away with the element of unfair surprise in a trial. Initially, discovery was hailed as a boon to truth seeking, fairness, and the expedited disposition of cases. No longer. Discovery abuses now constitute the single greatest source of dispute, delay, cost, and trickery in the adversary system. Excessive discovery tactics either bully the opposition into submission or limit and distort the flow of information. Either result defeats the principal purposes for which discovery was designed. . . .

Pretrial adversarial excesses continue during voir dire (jury selection), a fertile area for trial attorneys to ply their trade. Attorneys may dismiss prospective jurors by challenges. Those whose responses to the voir dire questions indicate probable bias are challenged for *cause*. Attorneys may perceive that other prospective jurors would not view their client's case favorably but are not sufficiently biased to challenge for cause. Such individuals can be removed by *peremptory* challenges. Unlike challenges for cause, peremptory challenges require no stated reason by the requesting attorney; however, they are limited in number—a common number is six for each side. But in cases of serious crimes, the number may be twelve or more. (There were twenty in the Simpson case.) Because of their limited availability, a premium is put on the attorney's skill in using peremptory challenges. . . .

TRUTH CORRUPTION

Once trial begins, tricks by attorneys can escalate—thanks in large part to the bench's historically lax enforcement of professional conduct rules. When infractions occur, they are routinely winked at by judges and bar association ethics committees. As a result, trial lawyers ostensibly enjoy a unique privilege in plying their trade: They are largely unanswerable to society for behavior that would be morally questionable elsewhere. This led the venerable jurist Felix Cohen to lament: "How the edifice of justice can be supported by the efforts of liars at the bar and ex-liars on the bench is one of the paradoxes of legal logic which the man on the street has never solved."

Space does not permit even a modest catalog of truth-corrupting tactics, but mention of a few common artifices will suffice:

Coaching witnesses. A standard practice is for attorneys to interview their witnesses in preparation for testimony. The practice is known by a variety of sobriquets—"rehearsing," "horse shedding," "prepping," and "sandpapering"—but the most common term is "coaching." The dangers of coaching are substantial: An attorney who knows the testimony of all friendly witnesses can orchestrate a common story that can avoid contradictions. In the course of coaching their witnesses, attorneys suggest "better" answers that, if not clearly contravening the witness' intended answer, subtly but effectively shade, dissemble, or distort the truth. The Simpson prosecutors continued to accuse the defense counsel of coaching those defense witnesses whose changed stories benefited the defendant.

BARRIERS TO THE TRUTH

We want to believe that the search for justice walks hand in hand with the search for truth, and surely our courts pay lip service to that value. Every day, in thousands of courtrooms across America, lawyers stand before judges and juries and proclaim, "We are not afraid of the truth." With utmost sincerity they promise, "We are here to seek the truth." O.J. Simpson's attorney Johnnie Cochran could look downright pious when he spoke of his concern for the truth. But every day he and his colleagues skimmed the edge of ethics to paint elaborate theories that strained an ordinary person's judgment and common sense.

In reality, the law is not necessarily a search for the truth. Indeed, it is often not a search for the truth. Our system is a carefully crafted maze, constructed of elaborate and impenetrable barriers to the truth. Even when the evidence against the accused is as clear as a ringing bell, lawyers will grasp at anything to fog the issues and mask the terrible facts.

Harold J. Rothwax, Guilty: The Collapse of Criminal Justice, 1996.

Attorney statements. Judges frequently tell jurors that attorney statements are not evidence. That is not enough. Jurors should also be informed that *attorneys are not under oath and do not have to believe their own statements.* Few jurors appreciate this. That is why attorneys are so effective when they (permissibly) impeach the credibility of witnesses they know to be telling the truth.

Similarly effective is the presumptuous question, one of the more insidious tools in the cross-examining attorney's arsenal. The presumptuous question implies a serious charge against the witness for which the attorney has little or no proof. An example: "Isn't it true that you have accused men of rape before?" Such innuendos are particularly effective against expert witnesses. A recent study found that by merely posing these questions, an attorney could severely diminish an expert's credibility, *even when the witness denied the allegation and his attorney's objection to the charge was sustained.* This clearly indicates that the presumptuous cross-examination question is a dirty trick that can sway jurors' evaluations of a witness' credibility.

Explanations for the effectiveness of this tactic vary. Communications research suggests people believe that when a speaker offers a premise, he has an evidentiary basis for it. With their pristine mind-sets, jurors assume that the derogatory premise of an attorney's question is supported by information. Another explanation lies in the possible confusion of jurors as to the sources of their information. The longer the trial, the less likely jurors will be able to distinguish information suggested by an attorney's presumptuous question from that imparted by the witness' answer.

Witness abuse. Cross-examining attorneys often regard witnesses as if they were open garbage cans and treat them accordingly. Early in the Simpson trial, for example, the defense resorted to hardball tactics against witnesses. Recall the derisive browbeating of police detectives by defense counsel. And when Simpson's friend, Ron Shipp, testified that O.J. had disclosed his dream of killing Nicole, the defense counsel on cross-examination accused Shipp of being an alcoholic, a deadbeat, an ingrate, and a perfidious grasper who knowingly betrayed his friend to advance his own aspirations as an actor. . . .

Emotional appeals. An emotional appeal to the jury, of course, is the time-honored ploy of the trial attorney with a weak case. How it will "play with the jury" becomes the overarching consideration in presenting evidence. Surely one of the most emotional moments in the Simpson trial appears to have been skillfully choreographed by the prosecution to have maximum impact on the jury. Assistant District Attorney Christopher Darden questioned Denise Brown, the sister of Nicole Brown Simpson, on the first Friday afternoon of the trial. After recounting O.J.'s past physical abuses of Nicole, Denise dissolved in tears. Darden then immediately asked for and received a recess, knowing that the jurors would carry that last compelling tableau with them over the entire weekend.

Adversarial trials conduce such drama because they are staged like theatrical performances. The show is the action taking place in the arena, bounded on the jury's right by the witness stand and judge's bench, and on the left by the attorneys' tables. Indisputably, the attorneys are the performers. Only they are allowed to walk freely in the arena, to and from the witness stand, the bench, and the jury box. They gesture, flail, and point. But mostly they talk: They bluster, blather, harangue, sermonize, and beguile. They laugh, cry, and bristle; they make the jurors laugh, cry, and bristle. Bar associations unabashedly offer "courtroom acting" classes to attorneys that satisfy continuing-education requirements. It is the greatest show in town because it involves real people with real problems and high stakes: prison or freedom; child custody or childlessness; recompense for serious bodily injury or destitution and welfare. Should matters of such consequence be resolved by a process that elevates showmanship over dispassionate and rational inquiry?

Dumb shows. The "repeated interruptions and disruptive tactics" referred to in the Los Angeles survey can come in many forms. Sometimes referred to as "dumb shows," this category consists of indecorous behavior intended to distract or mislead the jury, such as dropping books or making bogus objections. The legendary Clarence Darrow used a novel subterfuge. Before trial, he would insert a nearly invisible wire in his cigar. When his opponent began interrogating a witness, Darrow would smoke the cigar. Eventually, all eyes would follow the cigar ash, which, magically, never dropped.

Changing the story. In the unique, "fact-finding" inquiry that is the trial, attorneys selectively present evidence only to the extent that it furthers their version of the facts. The objective is to craft a credible story for the jury. In developing its story, the Simpson prosecution team chose an interesting strategy. Knowing it had to tarnish an American icon, the prosecution eschewed the conventional wisdom of beginning its case with evidence of the murder in favor of presenting evidence of antecedent wife beating.

AN UNFOLDING STORY

Sometimes the attorneys' stories change as the trial progresses. An Arizona trial judge offers his impression of how this happens:

> The sporting lawyer's concern is whether the story is convincing, whether it adequately meets the opposing story, not whether it is true or false. Thus it is not at all unusual to hear a courtroom story unfold like a novel, changing as the trial proceeds. Sometimes the story becomes clearer, sometimes fuzzier, sometimes contradicted as it is orchestrated by the lawyer-maestros. As one side crafts a story, the other side expresses outrage at the opponent's fiction and responds by fictionalizing its own story. The story is not as dismaying as the attorney's acquiescence in it. In this sort of liar's paradise, truth ceases to be a Heidegerian revelation; instead, trial evidence becomes a progressive sedimentation, with new layers of lies overlaying the original ones.

The defense's story certainly changed in the Simpson trial. Defense counsel Robert Shapiro initially said O.J. was asleep at the alleged time of the murder. Later, defense counsel Johnnie Cochran claimed O.J. was swinging golf clubs in his yard at that time. We can only speculate as to why the story changed. We know the change occurred after the judge ruled that O.J.'s exercise videotape—recorded shortly before the murders—could be shown to the jury. This evidence would obviously refute the claim that O.J. was so racked with arthritis at the time as to be incapable of a double murder with a knife. Once the arthritis claim was dropped, there was no disadvantage in maintaining O.J. was swinging golf clubs at the time of the murder. Further, it helped explain why O.J. was outside his house when he called his girlfriend on his cellular phone.

Partisan expertise. Will technological advances improve trial truth seeking? Even with the advent of more accurate fact-finding techniques such as DNA testing, the adversarial process will continue to subvert the truth by subordinating it to competing values. Peter Sperlich, who writes on the use of scientific evidence, says: "The adversary system maximizes the opportunities to obscure the facts, coopt the experts, and propagandize the judge. . . . The greatest single obstacle to complete an accurate scientific information . . . is the adversary system."

When expert witnesses are pushed into advocacy roles, attorneys and the system corrupt the value of the witness' expertise. Attention is too often focused on the personal characteristics of expert witnesses instead of the quality of their evidence. In a 1987 book compiling papers and comments on social research and the courts, the authors reached consensus on these points: (1) scientists serving as expert witnesses must expect to be used (and misused) for partisan purposes; and (2) the adversary system is not a reliable means of bringing all the relevant scientific data to the adjudicator's attention or of separating valid research from unwarranted conclusions.

With judges being generally passive, the scope of zealous advocacy trial tactics is limited only by the often-fertile imaginations of the litigation attorneys. Censuring individual practitioners or even the entire litigation bar for this state of affairs misses the source of the problem. After all, trial lawyers merely play their assigned roles within the adversary system. We should not condemn the attorney for engaging in morally questionable but nevertheless permissible trial tactics. Rather, we should decry the system that sanctions such tactics.

> "The criminal trial is flawed because
> it is not adversarial (or at least not
> as adversarial as it should be)."

THE CRIMINAL TRIAL SHOULD BE
MORE ADVERSARIAL

Kenneth B. Nunn

According to Kenneth B. Nunn, justice does not exist in the
American criminal justice system. In the following viewpoint,
Nunn argues that the criminal trial—the centerpiece of the
flawed justice system—should be more adversarial to protect
defendants. Nunn believes that while society professes a presumption of innocence, in reality, the cultural attitude is that the
defendant is always guilty and the preferred outcome of any
criminal trial is conviction. In this environment, Nunn charges,
the prosecutor has marked advantages over the defense, which
often has a difficult time convincing a jury of a defendant's innocence. To yield a fair trial, Nunn contends, the criminal trial
must bolster the adversarial stance between defense and prosecution so that the defendant can effectively combat the allega-
tions against him or her. Kenneth Nunn is an assistant professor
of law at the University of Florida law school.

As you read, consider the following questions:

1. What cultural messages are communicated to jurors,
   according to Nunn?
2. According to Nunn, why is the adversarial system the
   "linchpin" of the criminal justice system?
3. According to the author, why are a defendant's trial rights
   central to the notion of an adversarial system?

From Kenneth B. Nunn, "The Trial as Text; Allegory, Myth, and Symbol in the Adversarial
Criminal Process," *American Criminal Law Review*, vol. 32, no. 3 (Spring 1995), p. 743.
Reprinted by permission of the publisher, Georgetown University, and *American Criminal
Law Review*; ©1995.

It is a recurring image on our television screens: a young man—frequently Black and poor—is hustled from police car to courthouse door. As two burly police officers grip him tightly by the arms, he tries to hide his face with his hands. His efforts are futile. He succeeds only in exposing his handcuffs to the bright television lights. In the background, a reporter's urgent voice describes the despicable act which led to the young man's capture. His anguished face, framed by gleaming handcuffs, is the garish image we remember.

When I was a public defender, I would watch episodes like this with dread. "What if," I would wonder, "that young man was to become my client at the next day's arraignment call? Could I be of any help to him? Or would I be essentially useless, since he had already been tried and convicted on television and in the hearts and minds of any potential jurors?" Certainly, I could do something. I could ameliorate the onslaught of state power by holding the government to its promises and making sure no shortcuts were taken. Occasionally, in an exceptional case, I might even win an acquittal. But, by and large, in case after case, my presence has had little bearing on the outcome. In the vast majority of cases, the conclusion was foregone, the conviction assured, the case open and shut. I was a necessary, but irrelevant, player in a game with a predetermined outcome.

A FEEBLE CRIMINAL JUSTICE SYSTEM

We Americans often speak of our criminal procedure as if it were one of the main bulwarks of democracy. We like to consider the criminal trial, with its adversarial process, as one of the great institutions of abstract justice. But the American criminal justice system is a sham. The centerpiece of the criminal justice system—the trial—is itself a sham. It is not, in the main, a mechanism for determining the truth. In the majority of criminal cases, the truth is already assumed from the start. While belief in the presumption of innocence is professed, the defendant is treated as if his guilt were assured. In reality, it is up to the defendant to prove, if possible, his innocence and to somehow show that he is an exception to the rule.

More concretely, the criminal trial is flawed because it is not adversarial (or at least not as adversarial as it should be). Instead of two evenly matched adversaries, the advantages are decidedly weighted in the prosecution's favor. The prosecution has tremendous resources at its disposal that are ordinarily not available to the defense: police investigators, government laboratories, a professional legal staff, an endless supply of expert witnesses and, most importantly, a far greater reserve of credibility. This imbalance is even greater when the defendant is represented by a public defender. This is doubly cruel because the defendants who are at greatest risk in the criminal justice process—those with the least personal resources—are the ones most likely to be represented by public defenders.

Of course, the defendant has the protections of the Fifth and Sixth Amendments—including the right to a fair trial, the right to effective assistance of counsel, the right against self-incrimination, the right to compulsory process, the right of confrontation, and the requirement of proof beyond a reasonable doubt—but these are, by and large, merely formal protections. How defendants are treated in fact is what is important, not simply abstract theory. To have any relevance, the formal protections afforded to defendants must be appraised in the cultural context which gives them meaning.

Trials take place within a culture, a culture which gives us certain ideas about the prosecution and certain opinions about the defendant. Every culture produces its own belief system. This belief system is transmitted to each member of society through such means as formal educational systems, media, authoritative pronouncements and word of mouth. A cultural belief system allows us to attach meaning to symbolic representations that appear in culturally determined contexts. Thus, the imagery of the courtroom—the "dignity" of the proceedings, the "impartiality" of the judge, the adversarial posture of the litigants—and the juxtaposition of symbols of authority—the flag, the judge's black robe, the police officer's badge—all communicate culturally determined meaning to prospective jurors. There should be no mystery as to what meaning it is that the criminal justice system communicates to the American public. Our society is one where jurors are taught repeatedly, through both obvious and subtle means, that the preferred outcome of any trial is the conviction of the accused. In an environment such as this, a requirement of proof beyond a reasonable doubt is of little value.

DEFENDANT AS CRIMINAL

The image of the accused presented in criminal procedure books—that of an average citizen, who is merely "suspected" of crime, and who consequently retains his rights and social status until the state meets a heavy burden of proof—is a widespread fraud. Instead, the defendant plays the mythical role of "criminal" in a broader morality play, the well-known script of which allows the audience to boo and hiss as soon as the villain enters the scene. The defendant in a criminal case is supposed to lose, just as a villain in a Hollywood movie is also supposed to lose. More often than not, a criminal trial consists merely of two groups of actors playing their appointed parts—the prosecution in white hats, the defense in black.

The criminal trial, then, is an allegorical tale disclosing the way that society would like to discover, expose and exorcise crime. As allegory, the trial does more than merely determine the fate of the defendant standing trial, although it does that too. The trial represents something deeper. The trial expresses fundamental notions about justice and injustice, right and wrong, law-abiding and crime, good and evil. Within the confines of this allegory, the public defender's role is essentially symbolic. The public defender demonstrates that justice is being done and that the trial is fair. Symbolically, it matters little whether the public defender can actually assist the defendant because, as a mythical "criminal," the defendant is always guilty. . . .

THE ADVERSARY SYSTEM

The adversary system is a carry over from the English common law. The system is not mentioned in the Constitution. Nor is it preserved, by and large, by statute. Yet, the adversary process is the linchpin of our criminal justice system. A person charged with a crime is not just the accused, but the *defendant*—someone who retains the capacity to combat and contest the government's accusations.

The adversary system receives praise from many quarters because, it is argued, the self-interest of the parties will motivate them to more thoroughly prepare their submissions to the fact finder than if a more dispassionate investigator were charged with the responsibility. Also, it is assumed that a disinterested fact finder is less likely to show bias because he or she has no vested interest in the way that the investigation is conducted or how trial preparations are made. The adversarial system works on the assumption that truth will prevail from the conflict between two opposing forces.

Within the adversary system, the criminal defendant is entitled to an impressive array of rights. The most important of these, from an adversarial standpoint, is the right to counsel, for it is through counsel that the defendant is best able to exploit the adversarial process and champion his cause. The right to counsel originates in the Constitution. In *Gideon v. Wainright* the Supreme Court read the Sixth Amendment to require that counsel be provided to indigent criminal defendants in felony cases at state expense. Later, the Supreme Court interpreted the indigent's right to appointed counsel to be applicable in all cases in which actual imprisonment was imposed, as well as to appeals as of right. In other cases the Court broadened the right to counsel to require state provision of expert witnesses, trial transcripts, and other "basic tools of an adequate defense." Finally, courts have made some effort to address the quality of legal services provided to criminal defendants. On the surface, then, the obligation of the state to provide legal assistance to those who are too poor to secure their own defense seems quite extensive.

PROSECUTORIAL ADVANTAGES

Both prosecutor and defense attorney are legally obligated to argue their cases to the best of their abilities, each substantiating their arguments with the evidence that their side possesses. In theory, the truth is supposed to reveal itself as both counselors argue their cases before an objective body. This theory is based upon the assumption that both sides possess comparable abilities and also have equal access to resources. This was the intent of our forefathers, but is not at all the case today.

Prosecutors have many advantages over defendants in today's courtrooms. Over ninety percent of all accused persons are relegated to enlisting the services of a public defender for their trials. Although both prosecutors and public defenders are funded by the same source, the money allocated to both sides is far from equal. While prosecutors are afforded flexibility in funding the preparation of their cases, the State Public Defenders Office is allotted a fixed amount which must be divided amongst all their clients. In many cases, public defenders are unable to conduct research into alternative theories of a case simply because they do not have the financial resources to do so.

Alan Orfi, *Prison Mirror*, February 1, 1995.

There are other rights that a defendant may claim to help bolster his or her defense. A defendant has a right to be present at trial, the right to confront the witnesses against him or her, and the right to cross-examine those witnesses. The defendant also has the right to present a defense and the right to compulsory process in order to obtain witnesses or evidence. Furthermore, the defendant has a right to testify and a right to remain silent. Finally, the defendant has a general right to fairness in the prosecution of his or her case—i.e., the right to due process of law.

Many of the aforementioned rights would only make sense within an adversarial process. For example, in a non-adversarial process a defendant would need no right to present a defense, and a right to remain silent would seem incongruous. The purpose of the defendant's trial rights is to place the defendant on an even footing with the prosecution so that he or she might be a more effective adversary to the prosecution.

The presumption of innocence and the requirement of proof beyond a reasonable doubt are also central to the notion of an adversarial system of justice and are considered to provide additional protection for the criminal defendant. The presumption of innocence is implied by the accusatorial structure of the criminal justice system. It holds that the burden of proof is on the government and absent sufficient proof, the defendant must go free. In the adversarial framework, the defendant has no obligation to produce evidence of his or her innocence.

Proof beyond a reasonable doubt is the burden the government is required to meet in order to obtain a conviction. It is a "heavy" burden of proof, the highest such standard in the criminal justice system. The burden of proof beyond a reasonable doubt is intended to provide protection against erroneous convictions. In principle, a burden of proof beyond a reasonable doubt moderates the adversary system and makes it more responsive to individual rights.

Taken together, the formal rights extended to criminal defendants, along with the presumption of innocence and the requirement of proof beyond a reasonable doubt, constitute a "myth" that permeates the criminal justice system and defines how the system is envisioned. In short, the myth proceeds along these lines: A defendant who is presumed innocent must be proven guilty beyond a reasonable doubt at an adversarial trial that is fair and at which he or she has counsel. The basic assumptions behind the myth (that is, the points that the myth seeks to validate) are: (1) the existence of formal rights adequately protects the individual from the state and (2) because these formal rights make it difficult for the state to secure convictions in an adversarial context, those convictions that do occur are "hard won" and thus more legitimate. The function of the myth, then, is to bestow peace of mind by encouraging the belief that justice is being done in the criminal justice system.

| "The Bill of Rights and an attorney's rules of professional conduct require . . . that anyone accused of a crime is entitled to a lawyer."

A CASE FOR DEFENDING THE GUILTY

Robert L. Shapiro

Robert L. Shapiro was a key member of the O.J. Simpson legal defense team in the highly publicized "trial of the century." Simpson's not guilty verdict left many questioning whether overzealous attorneys allowed a guilty defendant to elude punishment, fueling nationwide debate about the role of defense attorneys. The following viewpoint is excerpted from Shapiro's book *The Search for Justice: A Defense Attorney's Brief on the O.J. Simpson Case,* in which Shapiro argues that defense attorneys must vigorously defend all citizens, even those who appear guilty. Because fear of crime is high, Shapiro contends, society often demeans defense attorneys because they advocate the rights of those who may pose a menace to society. But this advocacy, Shapiro contends, is crucial, for it preserves the safeguards—including the right to defense—that protect all citizens.

As you read, consider the following questions:

1. According to Shapiro, what do an attorney's rules of professional conduct require?
2. How do the roles of prosecution attorneys and defense attorneys differ, according to the author?
3. In Shapiro's opinion, how does the media shape public perception of defense attorneys?

The most frequent question a defense attorney is asked (and this goes double for one involved in high-profile criminal cases) is "How do you sleep at night?" I heard it myself almost daily during the O.J. Simpson trial, especially when the prosecution was presenting its case and the evidence against my client was mounting. The second thing I heard, especially from people who know me well and feel comfortable leaning on me just a little harder, was "In your heart, don't you know he did it?"

My answer to the second question is simple: "I wasn't there, you weren't there. Ultimately, it is a matter to be decided by the court."

My answer to the first question—How do I sleep at night?—is a little longer.

We live in a nation founded on the principles of freedom and liberty. We fought dearly for those principles, and we pay a continuing price. The Constitution—and, in particular, the ten amendments that make up the Bill of Rights—is where that price is clearly set out, in plain and simple English. Of those first ten amendments, five are specific as to the rights of citizens who find themselves in an adversarial relationship with the judicial process: the Fourth Amendment protects the people against unreasonable search and seizure; the Fifth sets out the protections of due process, including self-incrimination; the Sixth ensures a public trial and the assistance of counsel; the Seventh guarantees the right of trial by jury; and the Eighth prohibits cruel and unusual punishment. It is the provisions in this document and nothing else—not good intentions, not patriotism, not capitalism, not orthodoxy—that stand like a sentry between us and our becoming a police state.

THE RIGHT TO COUNSEL

The Bill of Rights and an attorney's rules of professional conduct require (they do not *suggest*) that anyone accused of a crime is entitled to a lawyer, as well as a trial. A defense attorney's job is not to "get someone off" but rather to represent someone's interests when the formidable resources of the state are arrayed against that person. And we aren't allowed to adjust our efforts to fit the circumstances, no matter the crime, no matter how morally questionable the person accused of it may appear to be, no matter our public or private assumptions of that person's guilt or innocence. A surgeon doesn't do less than his best when he's confronted with a person he detests on the operating table; neither does a lawyer. They *cannot*: Their respective professional codes of ethics forbid it. In my home state of California, the

Business and Professions Code Section 6068(h) expressly forbids an attorney "ever to reject, for any consideration personal to himself, the cause of the defenseless or the oppressed."

Prosecution attorneys and defense attorneys are officers of the court, both bound by the same rules of evidence and the same rules of professional conduct. However, our advocacy roles are different. The prosecutor's responsibility, according to the American Bar Association's Code of Professional Conduct, is "to seek justice, not merely to convict." The defense attorney's responsibility is "to represent his client zealously within the bounds of the law." The resulting adversarial presentation "counters the natural human tendency to judge too swiftly in terms of the familiar that which is not yet fully known."

INTERPRETING THE LAW

When a client says "I'm guilty," what he means is "I'm responsible"—for setting in motion certain events that culminated in a crime or act of violence. To the public, a defendant is either guilty or not guilty. But a criminal attorney recognizes that the law is not black and white—everything is shades of gray. In a death case, is it murder? Is it manslaughter? Or is it justifiable homicide? In a burglary, is it first-degree or second-degree? What is the difference between assault with a deadly weapon and assault with intent to commit murder? All have the same basic elements, but each has tremendously different legal consequences. It is up to the courts to ascertain the level of responsibility and the penalty, if any, to be paid for it.

Robert L. Shapiro, *The Search for Justice: A Defense Attorney's Brief on the O.J. Simpson Case,* 1996.

In *Berger v. United States* (1935), the Supreme Court stated that the prosecutor "is the representative not of an ordinary party to a controversy, but of a sovereignty . . . whose interest . . . in a criminal prosecution is not that it shall win a case, but that justice shall be done." Justice means different things to different people. There is legal justice and moral justice. When most people talk about justice, they're talking about moral justice. Did someone commit a crime or not? If so, that person should be tried, convicted, and punished. If not, he or she should be acquitted. As a defense attorney, however, I must view justice as our (that is, our country's) system of legal justice, which is based not on the assumption of guilt but on the presumption of innocence. Guilt must be proven by the prosecution. And it must be proven beyond a reasonable doubt and to a near certainty within the rules of constitutional law.

Reasonable doubt is a standard of common sense that is at the heart of our system of justice. Neither the prosecution nor the defense instructs the jury on that standard; the judge must do it. And judges have been wrestling with the intricacies and complexities of jury instruction, in both the state and federal courts, in nearly every single trial since the beginning of our criminal justice system. Ultimately, the questions before a jury are, Have they proved this case to your satisfaction? Are you sure? If someone near and dear to you—yourself, your relatives, your children—were on trial, and this type of evidence was presented against that person, would you be confident that you had made the right decision? Or would you be uneasy? Would you think, Did I do the right thing? Could I be wrong? If you're 90 percent certain, that still leaves 10 percent doubt. And if you have doubts—rational doubts, based not on speculation but on fact—then you have no right to convict. Judge William Blackstone anticipated society's struggle with this when he said, more than two hundred years ago, "It is better that ten guilty persons escape than one innocent suffer."

MODERN CRIME

Society has become so afraid of crime that Americans seem increasingly willing to forgo the Bill of Rights, convinced that it protects the sinners rather than the sinned-against. "Well, the Founding Fathers couldn't have foreseen gang wars," goes the rationale. Or crack, or insider trading, or contraband automatic weapons, or drugs, or sexual abuse, or pornography, or serial killers. To that, I would counter that neither could the Founders have envisioned the possibility that guilt or innocence might rest on a small laboratory slide containing an even smaller amount of deoxyribonucleic acid—DNA. Reasonable doubt takes on a new meaning in a case informed by science and determined by fallible human beings who interpret, manipulate, and define this data.

It's convenient, when confronted with the virulence of modern crime, to forget history, both ancient and recent, which is full of object lessons illustrating what happens when the rules that govern a people's conscience are, for whatever "expedient" reason, set aside. As the country's perception of crime goes up—and its intellectual understanding of the justice system correspondingly goes down—everybody decides that the solution to "the problem" is tougher sentencing, more jails, and bigger prisons. The results of that decision are questionable. Nationally, one-third of male African American adults ages eighteen to twenty-five are either in jail, on probation, or on parole. In California, the legitimate desire for safe streets has led to the "three-strikes-and-you're-out" law. However, most prosecutors and many judges have begun to feel that the system has been slowed down because of this law, as real menaces to society are put in a holding pattern awaiting trial while the court wrestles with the problem of the man with two prior convictions who's arrested for stealing a slice of pizza and now faces life imprisonment.

In the face of society's anger, it's almost inevitable that defense attorneys, rather than criminals, begin to carry the onus of crime. No longer seen as protectors of anyone's rights, or of constitutional rights, lawyers are hired guns, paid to "get the guy off," and the public doesn't care for us very much. That is, until that moment in many people's lives when they or someone near and dear to them is arrested for something as simple as drunk driving or as complicated as insider trading. And then the first question asked is "Where are my rights?"

Until and unless that moment happens, crime isn't committed by "us"; therefore, those accused of crimes aren't "us," and "they" are not entitled to the same constitutional protections that "we" are entitled to. Or, as one defense attorney once put it, "Everybody in town hates my guts—until two o'clock in the morning, when their kid gets arrested."

THE ROLE OF THE MEDIA

To be sure, defense attorneys have brought some of the criticism upon themselves, by their courtship of and relationship with the press. There's a natural symbiosis between big trials and the media, with both caught up in the playing-field drama of game plans, strategy, key players, winning and losing. The tremendous egos that motivate us to win in the courtroom are not immune to the adulation that comes outside as attorneys spin their successes, in the process becoming everything from talk-show staples to Sunday-morning-TV pundits. Little wonder that in this environment the "celebrity attorney" becomes a pop-culture icon. It's one thing to garner respect, congratulations, and praise from one's peers and friends; it's another thing entirely to glance up during a Lakers game and see one's face juxtaposed with Jack Nicholson's on the massive video screen in the Great Western Forum.

The "Dream Team" glitz shouldn't blind society to the fact that defense attorneys, in addition to zealously representing clients, also offer an ongoing and vital civics lesson in the rights of individuals. We cannot ignore the role of popular culture in shaping—or misshaping—public perceptions and expectations. Cop shows, both fictional and nonfictional, routinely portray illegal search and seizure, the physical abuse of suspects, and manipulation of evidence, all in the interests of "getting the bad guy" by the end of the hour, minus, of course, the time expended for commercials. But trials, and the people in them, are all too real. These days, anybody can accuse anybody of anything; indeed, in civil suits, anybody can *sue* for anything. What if a neighbor doesn't like you, or a business competitor wants to weaken you, and so files a false report of wrongdoing? What if your ex-wife calls the IRS and tells them you're cheating on your income taxes? Or your ex-husband calls the vice squad and tells them you're running a prostitution ring? Do you want the police coming into your home or office, going through your records, going through your closets, without a warrant? What happens if your spouse is killed and you have no immediate alibi? Suspicion always focuses on the surviving spouse, yet most of us could never account for all of our minute-to-minute whereabouts on any given day or date, especially during the times that we are alone. These days, an accusation is enough to destroy a life; an indictment and trial holds that life up to the examination and judgment of a society. A defense attorney's job is to see to it that the man or woman who stands under that scrutiny doesn't stand alone.

The "Dream Team"

The terms "Dream Team" and "Trial of the Century" didn't come from me, and I was never comfortable with either of them. My primary focus from the beginning of the Simpson case was to vigorously defend my client and to assemble a team of experts to strengthen that defense. Within a day or two it was clear that this would become a highly visible case, although I couldn't know at that point the degree to which the public would continue to demand information and coverage. I believed that the visibility would be good for two things: first, for lawyers (especially criminal lawyers, who have historically always been demeaned) to demonstrate how professional they can be, so that the public would come to understand what the real role of a criminal lawyer is; and second, to serve as some kind of positive symbol at a time when race relations were seriously frayed, especially in my own city. We had been through the Rodney King and Reginald Denny trials, and the riots and the soul-weariness that came with them. We had been through, in my lifetime, the promise of the civil rights movement, which now seems to have come undone. Perhaps, I thought, my being a white Jewish lawyer defending a black man accused of killing two white people, one of whom was Jewish, would strengthen what had become weakened. Perhaps a vigorous defense team that included a respected African-American attorney, and an equally vigorous prosecution team led by a Jewish woman and another black man, could somehow convey the message that the American system of justice is ultimately more important than any racial or religious element within it. Unfortunately, I was wrong on all counts. I was clearly, clearly wrong. Was I naive? Perhaps. But even now I would argue that optimism and idealism—which keep me in this business—are difficult to sustain without sustaining some naiveté as well.

I am not omniscient, and I have no better way of judging guilt or innocence than anyone else. However, I do know one thing for certain: Legally, the result of the trial is correct. This was a solid case of reasonable doubt, and I knew that before the trial itself ever began. Based on the evidence presented to this jury, "not guilty" was the only verdict that could have been returned.

That doesn't mean a significant number of Americans aren't sitting out there this minute thinking, "O.J. probably did it." But under our system, "probably did it" is not sufficient to convict someone. You cannot ask the question on one side of the coin—How does the defense attorney sleep, knowing that sometimes the guilty go free?—without confronting the question on the flip side: How could any of us sleep if innocent people were put away? Or executed?

I take pride in what I do. I am a professional, I have a constitutionally mandated job, and I work hard at it. Therefore, I'm able to function as a lawyer and survive as a human being. And so I sleep very well.

"Nothing in the canons of ethics of the American Bar Association says a lawyer has to represent everyone who comes to his door."

A CASE FOR NOT DEFENDING THE GUILTY

Vincent Bugliosi

In his book *Outrage: The Five Reasons Why O.J. Simpson Got Away with Murder*, prominent attorney and author Vincent Bugliosi describes why he believes the O.J. Simpson verdict was a terrible miscarriage of justice. In the following viewpoint, excerpted from *Outrage*, Bugliosi recounts why he himself would not have defended Simpson, a defendant he believes is unequivocally guilty of murder. While Bugliosi contends that the right to counsel is an unassailable right, and would not reject the cause of the defenseless, he contends that nothing in the canon of ethics of the American Bar Association requires an attorney to represent every potential client, guilty or innocent. Because so many attorneys are available and willing to represent seemingly guilty defendants, Bugliosi charges that it is both ethical and appropriate to eschew defending the guilty, especially when there are no substantially mitigating circumstances.

As you read, consider the following questions:

1. Why does Bugliosi reject the argument that idealism motivates most defense attorneys when they represent clearly guilty defendants?
2. Why did Bugliosi opt not to defend Dr. Jeffrey MacDonald, who was accused of killing his wife and two daughters?
3. Why is the author critical of the way in which Simpson's lawyers defended him?

During my radio and television appearances on the Simpson case, I was frequently asked if I would have represented Simpson. Since I knew he was guilty, I always responded I would not have.

Some have been disturbed by my not wanting to represent anyone charged with murder or any violent crime unless I believe him or her to be innocent or unless there are substantially mitigating circumstances. Isn't everyone entitled to be represented by an attorney, guilty or innocent? In fact, that's the idealistic chant often recited by defense attorneys as justification for representing even the most vicious criminals in our society. The concept is unassailable, but idealism is rarely what motivates lawyers who represent guilty defendants. They take the work because trying cases is their livelihood, and they are ambitious to advance their careers. These motivations, while perfectly proper, are clearly not idealistic.

DEFENDING THE DEFENSELESS

True idealism would be demonstrated in a hypothetical situation such as the following. Suppose a family is brutally murdered in a small town, and none of the five lawyers in town is willing to represent the suspect because the enraged citizens are all convinced of the suspect's guilt and no lawyer wants to be ostracized in the community for attempting to get the suspect off. Finally, one attorney steps forward and says, "I don't care what my friends at the Rotary Club and the First Baptist Church say. This is America, and everyone is entitled under the Sixth Amendment to our Constitution to be represented by an attorney."

That would be idealism. I, too, would represent a defendant—even one I believed to be guilty of murder—if I were the only lawyer available, because the right to counsel is a sacred right in our society and much more important than any personal predilection I might have. But this type of situation simply does not exist in a city like Los Angeles, where 35,000 lawyers stumble over each other's feet for cases. (For instance, when Charles Manson was charged with the Tate-LaBianca murders, over two hundred lawyers signed in to see him at the county jail, obviously for the purpose of seeking to represent him.) So I am free to follow my inclination.

Since nothing in the canons of ethics of the American Bar Association says a lawyer has to represent everyone who comes to his door, I choose not to defend anyone charged with a violent crime unless I believe he or she is innocent or unless there are substantially mitigating circumstances. (By the latter, I don't mean the question said to be asked about the victim by hard-bitten sheriffs in rural Texas at the start of any homicide investigation: "Did he *need* killing?") I investigate my own cases, and if I become satisfied in my own mind that the person is guilty, with no substantial mitigation, I routinely refer the case to other lawyers.

My position is not a matter of high ethics. It's more a matter of motivation. Let's take some vicious SOB who picks up young girls, sexually abuses and brutalizes them, then murders them and dumps them on the side of the road. What conceivable motivation could I possibly have to knock myself out working a hundred hours a week trying to figure out a way to get this type of person off?

NATURAL JUSTICE

I am also not unmindful of the fact that were I to secure a not-guilty verdict for one of these defendants I represented and he went out and did it again, I could rationalize all I wanted, but I would be partially responsible. If I had not deceived the jury the first time around, there would not have been a second murder.

In a nutshell, although I have never been a law-and-order fanatic—in fact, I'm suspicious of those who are—I do believe that those who have committed serious crimes should be severely punished, and I do not want to be in a position of actively seeking to thwart this natural justice.

One illustration of my dilemma in legal defense work was the case of Dr. Jeffrey MacDonald, the Princeton-educated former U.S. Army Green Beret who was accused of savagely stabbing to death his pregnant wife and two young daughters in their Fort Bragg, North Carolina, home one rainy night in March 1970. He was first charged with the murders that year, but the case against him was dropped because the evidence was insufficient. It was sometime in late 1973 or early 1974 that a close woman friend of MacDonald's came to my office in Beverly Hills and told me that the doctor, who was then working as an emergency room physician in nearby Long Beach, had learned he was about to be reindicted. She said the doctor wanted to know if I would be interested in representing him. We could talk about it, I said, if the doctor was innocent. I told her, "Tell him, though, that for starters I want him to take and pass a polygraph test." While waiting to hear from him, I telephoned the federal prosecutor handling the case in North Carolina and asked what he had against MacDonald. The prosecutor would not say very much, but did mention a few pieces of evidence to me, one of which was that fibers from MacDonald's blue pajamas had been found embedded beneath the fingernails of his two-and-a-half-year-old daughter. That evoked in my mind the horrifying scene of a little girl crying out, "Daddy, Daddy, no," as she reached out and struggled against her father while he stabbed her to death. That was enough for me. I wanted nothing to do with the case. Mac-Donald's lady friend called a week later anyway to say that he did not think it was necessary to take a polygraph as a precondition to my representing him. Convicted of the triple murder in 1979, he was sentenced to three consecutive life terms in prison.

CHANGING THE ROLE OF DEFENSE COUNSEL

Perhaps the rules of ethics should require defense counsel to ask the defendant whether he committed the crime. Under the current practice, most defense lawyers do not ask their clients this question. This practice is designed to preserve the option of putting the defendant on the stand, because the ethics rules state that a lawyer should not knowingly offer perjured testimony. This practice of willful ignorance about a client's guilt only seems to facilitate the guilty defendant's opportunity to commit perjury and the possibility of defense counsel's complicity.

Second, maybe defense counsel should be required to suggest to the defendant that although he is legally entitled to profess his innocence, the moral thing to do, if he is guilty, may be to admit his guilt and accept responsibility for his actions.

Joseph D. Grano, *Harvard Journal of Law & Public Policy*, Spring 1996.

My disinclination to defend a murderer also resulted in my electing not to represent former San Francisco supervisor Dan White for the 1978 assassination murders of Mayor George Moscone and Supervisor Harvey Milk when friends of White's from the San Francisco Police Department—White was a former officer—asked me to.

Those are the only two really big murder defendants who have ever come to me. Since my image is still that of a prosecutor, when people get in trouble with the law, I'm usually one of the very last people they think of.

O.J. SIMPSON'S DEFENSE

Just because I could never have defended O.J. Simpson for these murders since I know he committed them does not mean I'm critical of the lawyers who did defend him for having done so. What I am very critical about is in the *way* several of them went about doing it. It's one thing to defend someone you know is guilty, even defend him vigorously. Who can validly criticize such a lawyer? Our system of justice and jurisprudence not only allows but encourages this.

But inasmuch as the defense lawyers had to know Simpson was guilty of these two terribly brutal murders, I personally wonder how they could possibly have found it within themselves to go far beyond a vigorous representation, defending him with the same passion and fervor with which one would defend his own parents, wife, or children who were being charged with a serious crime.

Moreover, although it's perfectly proper to defend a guilty person by trying to poke holes in the people's case, you don't, for instance, deliberately violate the rules, as Cochran did when he argued throughout his opening statement (which is not allowed), and you don't, in your opening statement, refer to witnesses whose identity and statements have not been turned over to the prosecution (in violation of the law). More important, you don't accuse innocent police officers of framing your client for murder. You don't inject the transparently fraudulent issue of race into the trial, particularly when it's to the detriment, as it was with Cochran, of your own race. You don't object time and again during the prosecutors' final summations, in a concerted, unprofessional, and unethical effort to interrupt the flow of their arguments, therefore denying the people their right to a fair trial. . . .

To borrow a phrase from Henry Roth's novel *From Bondage*, in the ensuing years each of the defense attorneys in the Simpson case will have to "reconcile himself with himself." Unless, that is, as another novelist, Gertrude Stein, once said about Oakland, California, "there's no there, there."

| "When the defendant is guilty, the defense attorney's role is to prevent, distort, and mislead."

DEFENSE ATTORNEYS DISTORT THE TRUTH

Harold J. Rothwax

Harold J. Rothwax was a judge of the New York State Supreme Court. The following viewpoint is excerpted from his book *Guilty: The Collapse of Criminal Justice*, in which Rothwax condemns the adversarial criminal justice system for allowing defense attorneys to knowingly obfuscate the truth. Rothwax argues that in a court of law, only the prosecutor inhabits the role of truth seeker. In contrast, Rothwax charges, defense strategies bear little resemblance to the search for truth; in fact, they deliberately suppress or distort an accurate reconstruction of the facts. About 90 percent of defendants who go to trial are guilty, according to Rothwax, fostering a climate in which defense attorneys must resort to extreme—and often unethical—measures to protect their clients from a guilty verdict.

As you read, consider the following questions:

1. According to Rothwax, how are prosecutors held accountable for their actions?
2. Why does Rothwax say that the majority of defendants are "probably guilty" even though he supports the presumption of innocence at trial?
3. Why do defense attorneys attempt to provoke judicial error?

From *Guilty*, by Harold J. Rothwax. Copyright ©1996 by Harold J. Rothwax. Reprinted by permission of Random House, Inc.

The aspect of our criminal justice system that frustrates people the most is that it seems so rife with game playing. Too often, attorneys appear to be so involved with their own concerns that the issues of justice and fairness become secondary. Such behavior only encourages cynicism on the part of the public. And as an officer of the court, I have the unpleasant task of making sure that the games stay out of my courtroom. It's not always in my power to succeed. . . .

Presiding over my own courtroom, I sometimes feel as if I am the ringmaster in some gladiatorial arena. Theatrics, not truth, is the guiding principle. Strength is the ultimate test.

At a trial, we have two gladiators in the ring—the defense and the prosecution. The defense lawyer's only goal is to represent his client. His only interest is his client—not society, not the victim. This man, the defendant, is entitled to a champion who will say on his behalf everything that can be said in the hopes that through such a challenge we can be satisfied that the resulting product will be one that has integrity.

In a court of law, only the prosecution is assigned the task of seeking the truth. Since we know that truth is not the sole or even the primary objective, we give the side that's not seeking the truth ample opportunity to suppress the truth within the law.

How does that alter the relationship between the two sides? The prosecutor says, "I believe this man is guilty and I'm going to seek his conviction."

Given that, it's up to the defense attorney to decide how he wants to proceed. It's not always easy, because often defendants say they're innocent no matter how great the evidence against them.

PLAYING THE ODDS

It's a strength-testing process. The defense strategy has nothing to do with the truth. It has to do with the odds.

Sadly, the culture that the defense lawyer inhabits today is one that says it's okay to push the envelope, to brush against the ethical barrier and occasionally slip over. The temptation to be overzealous can be very great. Statistically, about 90 percent of the people who go to trial in this country are guilty. That puts defense lawyers in a situation where they're constantly representing guilty people. That's how the envelope gets pushed. That's where the line gets crossed between pure zeal and the excessive zeal that is designed to confuse, cloud, or hide the truth.

On the other hand, the prosecutor's life is a constant call to accountability. Every time a prosecutor makes a mistake and the defendant is convicted, the case may be called up on appeal. Too often, the appellate court, the arbiter of courtroom rules, reverses convictions based on a small mistake or a technical error. That's accountability!

The popular notion is that it's the prosecution's job to get a conviction, no matter what. But that has not been my experience. I remember an occasion when the head of the Trial Bureau, Nancy Ryan, came to see me in my chambers. She was preparing to try a case that seemed strong, and since she's a talented lawyer, she had a good chance of getting a conviction. But Nancy was disturbed.

"Quite frankly, Judge, I've got problems with this case," she told me.

"How so?"

"Well," she said, "it's a one-witness identification and that troubles me. You know, Judge, one witness comes in and says this is so, and I challenge her and I question her and I test her and she gives me the right answers. But I've got a feeling up my spine. There's something off about this case."

This was certainly an interesting turn of events! "So, what does your office do in that kind of a situation?" I asked Nancy.

"We have a policy that if one DA feels uncomfortable about prosecuting a case because the person may not be guilty, the case is reassigned to another DA. And if the other DA investigates it and feels the same way, the case will be dismissed. Even if it seems there's sufficient evidence to take to a jury. And if the other DA investigates it and feels it's a good case, the other DA will prosecute."

I was impressed with Nancy's honesty as well as with her integrity. It confirmed my faith in the way cases are prosecuted.

Although the defense and prosecution are considered enemies to the death in this gladiator ring we call the courtroom, it has almost always been my experience that prosecutors do not want to risk sending an innocent person to jail.

Nonetheless, it's not surprising that our current system of criminal justice would breed cynicism, since so much of the time it seems focused on everything but truth-seeking.

DOES TRUTH MATTER?

Viewed one way, from the very instant police officers place a citizen under arrest, that citizen embarks on a journey, aided and abetted by the Constitution of the United States, that was exquisitely designed to impede or prevent the truth from ever seeing the light of day. The reason for these protections is clear.

But I wonder: Have we diminished the value of truth to the extent that it no longer matters?

In the past thirty-five years, our courts have focused intently on the need for fairness; both sides in a criminal case must be free to contend vigorously for vindication, and must be assured of a fair and full hearing. But our adversarial system in its attention to fairness has spawned excesses—most notably, an excessive tolerance of efforts by the contestants to distort the truth.

In 1980, Marvin Frankel, then a federal district judge, wrote in a short book, *Partisan Justice*, that the "search for truth" in the courtroom "fails too much of the time." Frankel maintained that "our adversary system rates truth too low among the values that institutions of justice are meant to serve."

Is Frankel correct? If a trial is not a search for truth, what is its point? Is it not ultimately a waste of our time and our resources? These are deep and complex questions, but I assure you they are not abstract. There are few things more meaningful and more firmly rooted in our community life than the way the state interacts with its citizens—especially when that interaction is the result of a crime against the community.

Increasingly, I suspect that the real issue is not one of ethics but of structure. The way our adversarial system presently works not only *diminishes* the possibility of truth, it *encourages* and fosters excess on the part of the lawyers vying for the upper hand. The goal has become victory, not truth. Our courtrooms have become casinos, with a professional culture of misconduct so pervasive and so profound that it is often unrecognizable as justice. Because we have ceased to see it clearly, we have also ceased to question it honestly and rigorously.

"PROBABLY GUILTY"

There has been a lot of talk inspired by the O.J. Simpson case that perhaps police and prosecutors sometimes "rush to judgment"—conspire to bring a person to trial without having proper evidence. That has not been my experience. Indeed, it is a ludicrous proposition. If it is true that volume is the dominant existential reality of the criminal justice system, why would prosecutors undertake to charge persons whom they did not believe were probably guilty and then assume the burden of proving the charges?

Our entire system prior to a defendant going to trial is composed of a set of probability screens. Defendants don't just show up in court on a whim, railroaded by the system. By the time a person reaches trial, he has been deemed "probably guilty" several times—by the grand jury and by the court in preliminary hearings. It might shock your notion of justice to hear me say that the majority of defendants are "probably guilty." But if you think about it, you'll realize that that's preferable to saying that most of the people we arrest and bring to trial are "probably not guilty."

You might wonder, though, how we can presume a defendant is innocent when we say he is probably guilty. First of all, the presumption of innocence is a trial presumption—it does not relate to the earlier stages of the process. It is a way of stating that the burden of proof is on the People, not the accused; it is a way of telling the jury to keep an open mind, don't jump to conclusions prematurely and don't presume he's guilty because he's in the courtroom. It's a way of saying to the jury: "Be fair. The People have accused this man. Now, let's see if they can prove it." Note that no one pleads innocent, and no one is found innocent. Defense attorneys don't argue innocence, they argue reasonable doubt. (The average defense attorney might say that a trial is not a search for truth but a search for reasonable doubt.)

What the presumption of innocence does not mean is that the defendant is probably innocent. If that were the case, there would be no righteous grounds to make an arrest. It would be a police state where "probably innocent" citizens were arrested arbitrarily. Unless there existed some grounds for regarding a person legally guilty, it would be morally monstrous to bring a charge against him, indict and jail him, and compel him to undergo the ordeal and disgrace of a trial.

The best way to put it is this: The trial is the process by which we go from a reasonable probability or warranted suspicion of guilt supported by evidence to an assertion under law of legal innocence or guilt.

DISTORTING THE FACTS

Since most defendants are in fact guilty of some or all of the charges, the usual defendant on trial is yearning neither for an accurate reconstruction of the facts nor for an error-free trial. (That is not to question the standards of presumption of innocence or proof beyond a reasonable doubt; although most defendants are guilty, not all are, and we don't know in advance who is and who is not.) So, the defense attorney resists, demands, opposes, and objects more than the prosecution, and is more often overruled. With the intention of being overruled, a defense attorney will often seek to "seed the record" with error. Issues will be raised for no other purpose than to provoke error.

It is only a short step from seeding the record with error to judge baiting. Although our professional ethics would seem to forbid such behavior, there is no bright line between acceptable courtroom gamesmanship and misbehavior. And the defense attorney's guild has never publicly condemned the view, as Marvin Frankel puts it, that "A judge is, in season and in due measure, fair game." A victory gained by provoking judicial blunders is a victory all the same.

Although a judge is committed to the search for the truth, he is also required by the rules of the game to sit helplessly by while professionals are engaged in a clearly deliberate and entirely proper effort to frustrate the search.

Yet it is the judge, ultimately, who must control the courtroom, rein in the lawyers, and instill a sense of dignity and sobriety to the process. I truly believe that judges get the lawyers they deserve.

Five years ago, a colleague of mine did a study in which she put people in different courts throughout the city to determine how different judges processed felons. She had the occasion to watch the same lawyer before ten different judges. He was a different lawyer each time, depending on the standards a particular judge held him to. Judges control the courtroom—either by action or omission. They have a big responsibility.

But the lawyers have a responsibility, too. They can argue the issue before the judge, and the judge then has to decide it. It's simple—as long as the judge maintains authority. It shouldn't even be a problem because, like any other gamesmen, these gladiators truly want clear rules. I think they have a yearning for rules, for order, for discipline. But if the judge doesn't control the process, they'll fall out of line. . . .

There are many places we can look for a cure to the out-of-control adversary system. But perhaps the best place to start is with a serious reevaluation of the role of the defense attorney.

The role of the defense attorney is to zealously represent his client within the bounds of the law, to defend his client whether he is guilty or not guilty, and so to attack the accusing witnesses whatever the truth of those accusations may be.

But can we conceive—and *should* we conceive—of a system in which defense attorneys would be more willing to view themselves as part of a system of law, and less willing to see themselves as the alter ego of their client?

Society has conferred on the legal profession a monopoly over the rendition of legal services, and has delegated to it the power of self-regulation in the belief that lawyer domination and lawyer centrality in the trial process will best serve the public interest—yet that belief and that assumption has not been justified in the event.

Still, it is fair to ask whether the system serves the public interest.

ETHICAL QUESTIONS

In 1966, Professor Monroe Freedman, a leading ethics scholar, asked what he described as "The Three Hardest Questions" (of a criminal defense attorney):

1. Is it proper to cross-examine for the purpose of discrediting the reliability or credibility of an adverse witness whom you know to be telling the truth?

2. Is it proper to put a witness (including the defendant) on the stand when you *know* he will commit perjury?

3. Is it proper to give your client legal advice when you have reason to believe that the knowledge you give him will tempt him to commit perjury?

Professor Freedman answered all three questions in the *affirmative*—and thereby launched a storm of controversy that has yet to settle.

In twenty-five years on the bench, during which I have handled literally thousands of criminal cases, I have *never* been approached by a defense attorney plagued by *any* of these conundrums.

These are, unfortunately, everyday practices of the criminal defense lawyer. Freedman's questions were answered with ease and comfort a long time ago. And because they grow out of the confidentiality of the attorney-client privilege, they never reach visibility within the system. Only academicians—not courts—deal with these "hard" questions today.

We have never resolved the issue of the proper balance between zealous representation and the obligation of the lawyer to the court and to the public.

We may condemn the histrionics of lawyers as simply the tawdry business of amoralists doing what they find tolerable to earn a living. But this willingness to perform adversary stunts runs deeper than greed. It interferes with the very nature of the process.

The defense attorney cannot be just a "mouthpiece," but neither is he a public servant. He must be permitted and obliged to assert the rights that are available to his client under law.

Given the probability that the defendant is guilty, the defense attorney knows that the defendant will win *only* if counsel is successful in *preventing* the truth from being disclosed—or, failing that, misleading the jury once it is disclosed. So, when the defendant is guilty, the defense attorney's role is to prevent, distort, and mislead.

Our professional ethics and our procedural law are intertwined. Much of what appears at first to be an ethical question is actually a question about the wisdom of our rules of evidence and procedure, and the better course may often be to change the procedural rule.

| "The reality is that most defense attorneys are outstanding servants of their clients and the public good."

DEFENSE ATTORNEYS DO NOT DISTORT THE TRUTH

Charles M. Sevilla

Defense attorneys benefit the public good, according to Charles M. Sevilla. In the following viewpoint, Sevilla argues that society's tendency to demonize criminal defense lawyers is misguided, unfair, and undermines the protections of the Sixth Amendment, which guarantees a public trial and also the assistance of counsel. Sevilla believes that the system of checks and balances—such as rules of professional conduct that prevent falsifying evidence or lying in court—ensures defense attorneys' honest, ethical conduct. It is a myth, Sevilla contends, that defense attorneys seek to hide the truth, confuse jurors, or cause incorrect verdicts. Sevilla has been a criminal defense lawyer for twenty-five years, including thirteen as a public defender.

As you read, consider the following questions:

1. According to Sevilla, what historical examples support the contention that limiting the role of defense counsel endangers human liberty?
2. Why does Sevilla believe that independent defense counsel is crucial to the criminal justice system?
3. In the author's opinion, do defense attorneys commonly use exclusionary rules to free guilty defendants?

Reprinted from Charles M. Sevilla, "Criminal Defense Lawyers and the Search for Truth," *Harvard Journal of Law and Public Policy*, vol. 20 (Winter 1997):519, by permission of the publisher.

The task of defense lawyers is to defend their clients honestly and zealously under the constitutional mandate of the Sixth Amendment. This insures that the innocent are protected, that the state's search for truth is monitored, and that a balanced system results. Only in this way will society accept the end result as just.

Without doubt, defense lawyering is becoming increasingly difficult. Attacks on the independence of defense attorneys have become increasingly successful. These attacks are not new. Politicians have long focused on defense attorneys as the cause of the criminal justice system's problems, a criticism as meritworthy as blaming doctors for the incidence of cancer. Great leaders of our country who have worn the proud mantle of criminal defense attorney (e.g., John Adams, Daniel Webster, Abraham Lincoln) were similarly criticized in their day for their work defending citizens accused of crime. Indeed, back in the 16th century, Shakespeare suggested that one of the first steps toward despotism is the elimination of those who uphold the rule of law, when he had one of his would-be revolutionary characters suggest, "The first thing we do, let's kill all the lawyers." More recent history confirms this intuition. One only need look to Hitler's Germany to find a sophisticated society in which the role of the independent defense counsel was turned into that of toadying partner of the state. The architects of this change were some of the leading intellectuals of the day. For example, Heinrich Henkel, a professor of criminal law, wrote:

> By freeing ourselves from the notion of parties [to a lawsuit], we free ourselves from the liberal notion of a trial as a conflict of aims, an unleashing of a struggle to find the truth, which by its very nature as a conflict between two parties makes the finding of truth difficult. We thus become free to set against the liberal system of opposing forces a new order, in which the participants have a unanimity of aim.

Similarly, Dr. Alfons Sack, a criminal lawyer, urged judges, public prosecutors, and defense attorneys to be "comrades on the legal front . . . fighting together to preserve the law." He wrote:

> The coordination of their tasks must guarantee their practical cooperation and comradeship. . . . Just as the new trial no longer represents a conflict between the interests of an individual and the state, now the legal participants should regard their tasks no longer as opposed to one another, but rather as a joint effort infused with a spirit of mutual trust.

Men like these helped eliminate an independent defense bar in the Third Reich. With it, they assisted in the demolition of the rule of law and paved the way for world war and genocide.

Of course, eliminating defense counsel is not a goal unique to fascist regimes. As his communist regime crumbled in Romania, ex-President Ceaucescu fell victim to the injustice he had helped create. He was arrested, and trial was held immediately. During the hour-and-a-half-long trial, his assigned counsel successfully advocated the proper punishment for his client: death.

UNDERMINING THE RULE OF LAW

Such extreme examples of political systems gone bad teach that an important component in establishing a totalitarian state is eliminating the rule of law, and that this is best accomplished by undermining the role of independent defense counsel. The Framers of our Constitution knew that without someone to remind the system of its paramount dedication to the rule of law and human dignity, liberty would exist only at state sufferance. The Constitution thus preserves an important role for defense attorneys, who, like Socrates' gadfly, must constantly goad the state to do the right thing—acquit, find a lesser degree of guilt compatible with the facts, dismiss for reasons of police entrapment, or sentence justly.

The reactionary echoes of past attempts to endanger the rule of law by undermining the role of criminal defense lawyers are still heard today; indeed, they are increasing in volume. These forces, propelled by a mythology of their own making about the criminal system, are undermining the independence of defense counsel, and with it the guarantee of the Sixth Amendment and the rule of law. The false message spread by these forces demonizes defense counsel, trumpets anecdotal or unusual incidents as the "norm," and attacks the constitutional protections of the accused by characterizing these protections as dangers to the public safety. This message is a fear-based doctrine propagated by those who see constitutional rights as destructive tools of society's outcasts. It has had an impact.

For defense attorneys, the result of legislative, executive, and court decisions based on this mythology is that today there exists a huge distance between the promise of the constitutional right to counsel and its delivery. There is at work a process bent on converting independent defense attorneys into the "comrades" of state prosecutors. This process is simultaneously diluting important constitutional protections to the point of insignificance.

MYTHS ABOUT DEFENSE ATTORNEYS

The public believes in this false message, this media-propagated mythology about the justice system. But reality is far different.

Let us examine some of the components of this mythology in more detail.

Myth 1: *Defense counsel act with a license to lie their clients out of trouble.* The reality is that most defense attorneys are outstanding servants of their clients and the public good. The public is protected from miscreant counsel by rules of professional conduct that "prevent counsel from making dilatory motions, adducing inadmissible or perjured evidence, or advancing frivolous or improper arguments . . . ." These rules exist, as they should, to require honest conduct, an absolute prerequisite for any justice system to work. Furthermore, these rules are enforced by the ability of police, prosecutors, courts, or bar associations to discipline those who violate them.

UNMERITED CRITICISM

The O.J. Simpson double-murder trial has spawned a new—and unfortunate—industry for lawyers and law professors. They now do play-by-play trial commentary on television. Whether or not they have ever tried a case, these talking heads have a comment or criticism about anything and everything dealing with the Simpson case. . . .

Because of the commentary spewing from many of these "experts" about trial lawyers' lack of ethics, the system, in general, and criminal-defense attorneys, in particular, have been tainted with a broad brush of irresponsibility that will cause future jurors to doubt courtroom actions and motivations. This can only further undermine an already fragile system. Ultimately, persons charged with criminal conduct in future cases will suffer because this could affect their constitutional rights to a fair trial.

Howard Weitzman, *Los Angeles Times,* July 9, 1995.

Further, vigorous defense counsel, in the course of their defense of the citizen accused of crime, provide an important teaching function. For example, every police department in this country has learned that if it does not rid itself of, or at least appropriately discipline and retrain, rogue officers, then vigorous defense counsel will expose the truth about those officers and the fate of a case may hang in the balance. Another important lesson has been that sloppy police lab work will be exposed in the courtroom. As a result of such exposure in the O.J. Simpson case, crime labs throughout the United States underwent self-examination to insure the integrity of their process. Good defense lawyering casts light on dark corners of the criminal justice system to help keep it honest. Such self-examination and correction makes prosecution cases more accurate, stronger, and properly deserving of credibility and respect by the public. Without a zealous and independent defense, this cannot happen.

Myth 2: *Publicly appointed defense attorneys have abundant resources at their command, and are free to act independently.* In fact, the vast majority of the accused in this country are represented by appointed private counsel or public defenders. Both types of attorneys are paid by the government. As creatures of politics, both types are subject to political economics. Defending unpopular accuseds does not make for political influence or easy budget sessions with local Boards of Supervisors. Due to fiscal restraints and generally declining resources, the bright and energetic people in public defender offices often are not given the basic tools with which to do their work. Lack of access to investigators, experts, criminalists, computers, and support staff is often a major impediment to proper representation. With underfunded and overworked public defenders handling massive caseloads, the promise of the constitutional right to counsel and its delivery become two entirely different concepts.

Secondly, defense lawyers are not independent. Local governments in larger cities are creating multiple "alternative public defender" offices so that government offices will handle all indigent cases. This exclusion of the appointed private defense attorney is another threat to the Sixth Amendment. A government that employs all those who serve in the indigent defense system has the power to diminish both the quality and the independence of that system. Quality can be brought down by overloading the attorneys with cases. Independence can be blunted by a bureaucratic leadership more interested in the continuity of the defender office than in its underlying mission of representing its clients. Vigorous *independent* advocacy is necessary to keep the criminal justice system honest. A government takeover of all indigent defense is a threat to that goal.

Myth 3: *Defendants are bamboozling juries and thereby walking free.* In the O.J. Simpson case, we saw an unusual event—a trial by jury. The reality is that our adversarial system bears more resemblance to a confessional system of justice in which lines of defendants, escorted by their defense counsel, approach the altar of court to confess their sins openly and then obediently go to jail to pay their debt to society. In most cases, defense lawyers function like confinement brokers, plea-bargaining their clients into custody in a system which bears more resemblance to a settlement bureaucracy than an adversarial trial system. In California, for example, well over 90% of criminal cases are resolved by guilty pleas. In 1991–92, only 3.7% of felony cases actually reached a jury trial. If our system of justice truly were one where a jury trial was a sure "get-out-of-jail-free card," all guilty-pleading defendants would be terribly misguided, especially given the strong likelihood that at sentencing they will be sent to jail or prison.

Of course, guilty pleas may serve the search for truth. However, every time a quick guilty plea takes place, a system-check opportunity is lost. Conduct of the system's participants—police, prosecutors, judges, and the defense—goes largely unreviewed. Our court system today, typified by near unanimous guilty pleas and an overburdened public defender system, is one in which power is largely unchecked and where abuse is most likely.

Myth 4: Exclusionary rules are commonly used by defense attorneys to free the guilty. In fact, defense motions to suppress physical evidence and confessions are almost always denied. Therefore, while exclusionary rules serve an important role as the only means of teaching police the necessity of obeying the laws they enforce, they seldom have outcome-determinative impact on criminal cases. Yet, merely by bringing the motion and examining the officer's conduct under oath to determine if it complies with the law, the defense lawyer provides a key and valuable check on police misconduct. Indeed, exclusionary rules for constitutional violations are well worth the cost of an infrequent ruling banning the evidence from the court.

Myth 5: If the defense loses the trial, it will use a "legal technicality" to win on appeal. In fact, with all the defendants pleading guilty, there are not that many appeals. Moreover, of those few criminal appeals that "win," the vast majority are remanded for retrial. The few reversals that are ordered each year are not granted on mere technicalities—the appeals court usually must be convinced that the error at trial actually prejudiced the defendant's right to a fair trial. Finally, appeals provide another important check on the system's functioning, as the intensity of appellate review has direct impact on the integrity of the trial process.

Myth 6: Defendants are receiving light sentences and getting early parole. This myth is continually exploited by politicians seeking votes under the banner of getting tough on crime. The myth is almost sure to be perpetual—if tougher laws are passed and the crime rate still rises, then the political answer is even tougher laws. But the reality is that America today has a relatively harsh system of sentencing. Federal sentences can be, and often are, lengthy. Federal parole has been abolished. With mandatory minimum sentences, in many cases a judge has no power but to give a first-time drug defendant ten or twenty years. States are adopting "three strikes and you're out" laws, which can put a criminal behind bars for life for relatively minor crimes. The rise in mandatory sentencing schemes means that the defense has little influence in sentencing, and judges are fast losing theirs. This trend vests enormous power in the prosecution while undermining the authority of courts to render justice with which legislatures may disagree.

The success the media has had in pounding this myth into the public psyche has resulted in many new laws and court decisions that have created a highly efficient conviction-producing machine in which most accuseds are punished and the most serious offenses are punished severely. But the myth-makers say this is not true, or not true enough. They continue to push for increasingly harsh sanctions and seek to strip away more and more constitutional protections. By pandering to public fear and targeting opponents with the label of political death—"soft on crime"—they succeed in diminishing constitutional and statutory rights. Recent changes have diminished the scope of protection afforded by federal habeas corpus, public funding for capital cases, and jury voir dire. Each of these changes further limits the ability of independent defense attorneys to defend clients.

CONCLUDING THOUGHTS

The result of the process driven by the mythology described above is more individual injustice, more unchecked exercise of state power, and more unjust convictions. The very character of our criminal justice system is being altered, and the protections we as a people consider the essence of American fairness are being discarded. With no political or moral leadership willing to oppose—much less offset—this trend, the myth-makers are succeeding in dismantling the balance the criminal justice system once had. The costs to society, both monetary and constitutional, have been enormous, but largely unrecognized. Despite ever-increasing taxes, the public seems not to recognize the enormous monetary costs involved in living in a nation run by fear and myth, a nation that views incarceration as the panacea for all its problems. Public knowledge of what is happening may be delayed until citizens face even higher taxes to pay for the exorbitant costs of prison building programs, and lose their property to unjust forfeiture laws and their loved ones to criminal charges undefended by a strong, independent defense bar.

As the role of independent defense counsel is diminished, so too is the search for truth.

PERIODICAL BIBLIOGRAPHY

The following articles have been selected to supplement the diverse views presented in this chapter. Addresses are provided for periodicals not indexed in the *Readers' Guide to Periodical Literature*, the *Alternative Press Index*, the *Social Sciences Index*, or the *Index to Legal Periodicals and Books*.

Akhil Reed Amar	"When Truth Is the Loser: The Courts Are Allowing Legal Games to Overshadow the Search for Justice," *Washington Post National Weekly Edition*, April 24-30, 1995. Available from 1150 15th St. NW, Washington, DC 20071.
Paul J. Buser	"Legal Ethics Issues: What Guides Conduct of Attorneys?" *Quill*, April 1997. Available from 16 S. Jackson St., Greencastle, IN 46135-1514.
Lincoln Caplan	"Don't Ask, Don't Tell," *Newsweek*, August 1, 1994.
Amitai Etzioni	"On Making Lawyers a Bit More Socially Responsible," *Responsive Community*, Fall 1995. Available from 2020 Pennsylvania Ave. NW, Suite 282, Washington DC 20077-2910.
Tom French	"Ehics and Persuasion: Right Makes Might in the Courtroom," *Trial*, April 1995.
Joseph D. Grano	"The Adversarial-Accusatorial Label: A Constraint on the Search for Truth," *Harvard Journal of Law and Public Policy*, Winter 1997. Available from Harvard Law School, Cambridge, MA 02138.
William W. Hodes	"Ethics of Defending Guilty Clients," *National Law Journal*, May 29, 1995.
Michele Leavitt	"Defending the Guilty," *Humanist*, January/February 1997.
Alan Orfi	"Public Needs to Be Aware of Tactics Used by Prosecutors," *Prison Mirror*, February 1, 1995. Available from PO Box 55, Stillwater, MN 55082-0055.
William H. Simon	"The Ethics of Criminal Defense," *Michigan Law Review*, June 1993. Available from Hutchins Hall, Ann Arbor, MI 48109-1215.
David Stewart	"Uncertainty About Reasonable Doubt," *ABA Journal*, June 1994. Available from 750 N. Lake Shore Dr., Chicago, IL 60611.

FOR FURTHER DISCUSSION

CHAPTER 1

1. John Douglas uses examples of heinous criminals to support his argument that the death penalty is a just and moral response to violent crime. James McCloskey cites biblical passages to strengthen his argument that sentencing a criminal to death is morally repugnant. Which author presents his viewpoint most persuasively? Defend your answer, using specific examples from the viewpoints.

2. Jimmy Carter describes a racially polarized criminal justice system, with punishment focused on black offenders. As an example, he cites the fact that sentences for possession or sale of crack cocaine, which is abused more often by blacks, are harsher than those for powder cocaine, which is abused more often by whites. Do you agree that this sentencing disparity points to a racist justice system? Why or why not? What other examples does Carter use to support his view? Do you agree with his assessment?

3. Linda Chavez and Robert Lerner use statistics to support their argument that blacks are more likely than whites to escape conviction. Does their use of statistics make their argument more or less persuasive? Explain your answer.

4. Alan Orfi maintains that prisons should focus on rehabilitation so that inmates can successfully reenter society. Does the fact that Orfi is a prison inmate lend more or less credibility to his argument? Why or why not? Based on your reading of the viewpoints, do you think that Charles H. Logan would agree with Orfi's assessment that prison life is unduly harsh? Explain your answer.

CHAPTER 2

1. While both Sol Wachtler and Dan Lungren acknowledge the importance of constitutional protections for accused persons, they disagree on the extent to which they should be applied. Do you find that Wachtler's status as an ex-convict and Lungren's role as California's attorney general affect your assessment of their arguments? Why or why not? If so, explain in what ways their backgrounds influence your opinion concerning this issue.

2. Paul Cassell and Stephen J. Markman argue that the Miranda rule is not particularly effective at protecting a suspect from coercion. Susan R. Klein disagrees, maintaining that Miranda

is well tailored to guard against constitutional violations. Whose view do you find more accurate? Explain.

3. Morgan O. Reynolds advocates a repeal of the exclusionary rule, charging that it thwarts justice by allowing guilty criminals to go free. Carol S. Steiker agrees that the exclusionary rule is somewhat flawed, but she argues that it must be preserved and upheld. How does each author interpret the role of the exclusionary rule? Based on their arguments, do you think the exclusionary rule is necessary? Explain your answer, using examples from the viewpoint.

CHAPTER 3

1. David LaCourse cites statistics that suggest that a "three strikes" law has reduced crime in Washington State, while Joseph D. McNamara argues that crime rate reductions may not be directly attributable to "three strikes" laws. What evidence does each author give to support his viewpoint? Whose argument seems stronger? Defend your answer.

2. Vincent L. Broderick argues that mandatory minimum sentencing receives widespread support because it is advocated by politicians who pander to the public's fear of crime. Do you agree or disagree with Broderick's view that mandatory minimum sentencing may result in excessive sentences? Explain your answer, giving specific examples from the viewpoint.

3. Jay Apperson supports mandatory minimum sentencing laws as a powerful weapon against drug traffickers. As you consider Apperson's argument, do you find his background as a federal prosecutor relevant? Why or why not?

4. James Wootton contends that criminals should not be released from prison before they have served their entire sentence, while Marc Mauer maintains that this view is misguided. How does each author use statistics to strengthen his own argument? Whose use of statistics seems more convincing? Explain your answer.

CHAPTER 4

1. Kenneth B. Nunn maintains that a clash of opposing views by attorneys in trial court is fundamental to criminal justice, while Franklin Strier describes the court system as overly adversarial. Which of these views do you find more convincing? Explain your answer.

2. Vincent Bugliosi argues that lawyers may ethically refuse to represent clients they believe to be guilty. Based on your assessment of his viewpoint, how do you think Robert L. Shapiro

would respond to this view? After reading the viewpoints, do you believe that lawyers should represent anyone who seeks their services? Why or why not?

3. In his argument that defense attorneys often distort the truth, Harold J. Rothwax cites numerous concerns with defense strategies. Do you agree that these are valid concerns? Why or why not? Charles M. Seville maintains that defense attorneys are honest, ethical servants of the public good. Which author do you most agree with, and why?

ORGANIZATIONS TO CONTACT

The editors have compiled the following list of organizations concerned with the issues debated in this book. The descriptions are derived from materials provided by the organizations. All have publications or information available for interested readers. The list was compiled on the date of publication of the present volume; the information provided here may change. Be aware that many organizations take several weeks or longer to respond to inquiries, so allow as much time as possible.

American Civil Liberties Union (ACLU)
125 Broad St., 18th Fl., New York, NY 10004
(212) 549-2500 • publications: (800) 775-ACLU (2258)
fax: (212) 549-2646
web address: http://www.aclu.org

The ACLU is a national organization that works to defend Americans' civil rights as guaranteed by the U.S. Constitution. It provides legal defense, research, and education. Among the ACLU's numerous publications are the book *In Defense of American Liberties: A History of the ACLU*, the handbook *The Rights of Prisoners: A Comprehensive Guide to the Legal Rights of Prisoners Under Current Law*, and the briefing paper "Crime and Civil Liberties."

American Correctional Association (ACA)
4380 Forbes Blvd., Lanham, MD 20706-4322
(301) 918-1800 • (800) 222-5646 • fax: (301) 918-1900
web address: http://www.corrections.com/aca

ACA is composed of correctional administrators, prison wardens, superintendents, and other corrections professionals who want to improve correctional standards. The ACA studies the causes of crime and reports regularly on criminal justice issues in its bimonthly newsletter, *Corrections Today*.

American Criminal Justice Association (ACJA)
PO Box 601047, Sacramento, CA 95860
(916) 484-6553 • fax: (916) 488-2227
e-mail: acjalae@aol.com • web address: http://www.acjalae.org

The association was formed in 1937 by a group of law enforcement officers interested in upgrading their profession. Its purpose is to increase the educational standards of peace officers, raise public awareness about the goals of peace officer organizations, conduct research in the field of police science, and foster cooperation among law enforcement agencies.

American Judicature Society
25 E. Washington St., Suite 1600, Chicago, IL 60602
(312) 558-6900

The society is made up of lawyers, judges, law teachers, and government officials who promote effective justice and combat court delays. The society conducts research, offers a consulting service, and publishes the magazine *Judicature*.

Campaign for an Effective Crime Policy
918 F St. NW, Suite 505, Washington, DC 20004
(202) 628-1903 • fax: (202) 628-1091

Coordinated by the Sentencing Project, the campaign favors alternative sentencing policies. Its purpose is to promote information, ideas, discussion, and debate about criminal justice policy. The campaign's core document is *A Call for a Rational Debate on Crime and Punishment*.

Families Against Mandatory Minimums Foundation (FAMM)
1621 K St. NW, Suite 1400, Washington, DC 20006
(202) 822-6700 • fax: (202) 822-6704
e-mail: famm@famm.org • web address: http://www.famm.org
FAMM is an educational organization that works to repeal mandatory minimum sentences. It provides legislators, the public, and the media with information on and analyses of minimum-sentencing laws. FAMM publishes the quarterly newsletter *FAMM-gram*.

Justice Fellowship
PO Box 16069, Washington, DC 20041-6069
(703) 904-7312 • fax: (703) 478-9679
web address: http://www.justicefellowship.org
The Justice Fellowship is a national criminal justice reform organization that advocates victims' rights, alternatives to prison, and community involvement in the criminal justice system. It aims to make the criminal justice system more consistent with biblical teachings on justice. It publishes the brochures *A Case for Alternatives to Prison*, *A Case for Prison Industries*, *A Case for Victims' Rights*, and *Beyond Crime and Punishment: Restorative Justice*, as well as the quarterly newsletter *Justice Report*.

National Association of Blacks in Criminal Justice
North Carolina Central University
Criminal Justice Bldg., Rm. 106, PO Box 19788, Durham, NC 27707
(919) 683-1801 • fax: (919) 683-1903
web address: http://www.nabcj.org
Founded in 1972, this organization comprises criminal justice professionals concerned with the impact of criminal justice policies and practices on the minority community. It seeks to increase the influence of blacks in the judicial system. Publications include the quarterly *NABCJ Newsletter* and the bimonthly newsletter *The Commitment*.

National Center on Institutions and Alternatives (NCIA)

3125 Mt. Vernon Ave., Alexandria, VA 22305
(703) 684-0373 • fax: (703) 684-6037
e-mail: ncia@igc.apc.org
web address: http://www.ncianet.org/ncia (main website)
web address: http://www.sentencing.org (website for NCIA's special
        project, Coalition for Federal Sentencing Reform)

NCIA works to reduce the number of people institutionalized in prisons and mental hospitals. It favors the least restrictive forms of detention for juvenile offenders and opposes sentencing juveniles as adults and executing juvenile murderers. NCIA publishes the study *Darkness Closes In—National Study of Jail Suicides* and offers the book *The Real War on Crime*, published by HarperCollins.

National Criminal Justice Association (NCJA)

444 N. Capitol St. NW, Suite 618, Washington, DC 20001
(202) 624-1440
e-mail: ncja@sso.org • web address: http://www.sso.org

NCJA is a Washington-based nonprofit organization that assists state and local governments with issues concerning crime control and public safety. NCJA advocates comprehensive planning and coordination among criminal justice system components in policy development. It publishes the monthly newsletter *Justice Bulletin*.

National Institute of Justice (NIJ)

U.S. Department of Justice
PO Box 6000, Rockville, MD 20849-6000
(800) 851-3420 • (301) 519-5212
e-mail: askncjrs@ncjrs.org • web address: http://www.ncjrs.org

NIJ is a research and development agency that documents crime and its control. It publishes and distributes information through the National Criminal Justice Reference Service, an international clearinghouse that provides information and research about criminal justice. NIJ publications include the bimonthly *National Institute of Justice Journal*.

Police Executive Research Forum (PERF)

1120 Connecticut Ave. NW, Suite 930, Washington, DC 20036
e-mail: perf@intr.net • web address: http://www.policeforum.org

PERF is a think tank made up of police chiefs and criminal justice professionals. The organization is committed to improving policing practices through research, national leadership, and debate. PERF publishes the quarterly newsletter *Problem Solving Quarterly* and the bimonthly newsletter *Subject to Debate*.

The Sentencing Project

918 F St. NW, Suite 501, Washington, DC 20004
(202) 628-0871 • fax: (202) 628-1091

The project provides public defenders and other public officials with information on establishing and improving alternative sentencing programs. It promotes increased public understanding of the sentencing process and alternative sentencing programs. The project publishes the reports "Americans Behind Bars: A Comparison of International Rates of Incarceration" and "Young Black Men and the Criminal Justice System: A Growing National Problem."

Victims of Crime and Leniency (VOCAL)
PO Box 4449, Montgomery, AL 36103
(334) 262-7197 • (800) 239-3219 • fax: (334) 262-7197

VOCAL seeks to ensure that a crime victim's rights are recognized and protected. It believes the U.S. justice system goes to great lengths to protect the rights of criminals while discounting those of the victim. VOCAL has been responsible for introducing or supporting fourteen victims' rights bills, including the Victim's Bill of Rights which guarantees that victims will be notified prior to the release of prisoners convicted of crimes perpetrated against them. It publishes the quarterly newsletter *VOCAL Voice*.

BIBLIOGRAPHY OF BOOKS

Stephen J. Adler · *The Jury: Trial and Error in the American Courtroom.* New York: Times Books, 1994.

Akhil Reed Amar · *The Constitution and Criminal Procedure: First Principles.* New Haven, CT: Yale University Press, 1997.

David Austern · *The Crime Victim's Handbook: Your Rights and Role in the Criminal Justice System.* New York: Viking, 1987.

Robert M. Baird and Stuart E. Rosenbaum · *Punishment and the Death Penalty: The Current Debate.* Amherst, NY: Prometheus Books, 1995.

Herman Bianchi · *Justice as Sanctuary.* Bloomington: Indiana University Press, 1994.

Robert James Bidinotto, ed. · *Criminal Justice? The Legal System Versus Individual Responsibility.* Irvington-on-Hudson, NY: The Foundation for Economic Education, 1994.

David Bodenhamer · *Fair Trial: Rights of the Accused in American History.* New York: Oxford University Press, 1991.

Vincent Bugliosi · *Outrage: The Five Reasons Why O.J. Simpson Got Away with Murder.* New York: W. W. Norton, 1996.

Frank M. Coffin · *On Appeal: Courts, Lawyering, and Judging.* New York: W.W. Norton, 1994.

George F. Cole · *The American System of Criminal Justice.* Pacific Grove, CA: Brooks/Cole, 1989.

Christopher Darden · *In Contempt.* New York: ReganBooks, 1996.

Alan M. Dershowitz · *Reasonable Doubts: The Criminal Justice System and the O.J. Simpson Case.* New York: Simon and Schuster, 1997.

John J. DiIulio Jr. · *No Escape: The Future of American Corrections.* New York: BasicBooks, 1991.

Stephen A. Donzinger, ed. · *The Real War on Crime: The Report of the National Criminal Justice Commission.* New York: HarperPerennial, 1996.

R. Anthony Duff and David Garland, eds. · *A Reader on Punishment.* New York: Oxford University Press, 1994.

George P. Fletcher · *With Justice for Some: Victim's Rights in Criminal Trials.* Reading, MA: Addison-Wesley, 1995.

Lois G. Forer · *A Rage to Punish: The Unintended Consequences of Mandatory Sentencing.* New York: Norton, 1994.

Mansfield B. Frazier · *From Behind the Wall: Commentary on Crime, Punishment, Race, and the Underclass by a Prison Inmate.* New York: Paragon House, 1995.

Lawrence M. Friedman — *Crime and Punishment in American History.* New York, BasicBooks, 1993.

Jewelle Taylor Gibbs — *Race and Justice: Rodney King and O.J. Simpson in a House Divided.* San Francisco: Jossey-Bass, 1996.

Robert A. Goldwin and William A. Schambra, eds. — *The Constitution, the Courts, and the Quest for Justice.* Washington, DC: American Enterprise Institute, 1989.

Alan T. Harlan — *Choosing Correctional Options That Work.* Thousand Oaks, CA: Sage, 1996.

Joel H. Henderson — *Crime of the Criminal Justice System.* Cincinnati: Anderson Publishing, 1994.

Bruce Jackson — *Law and Disorder: Criminal Justice in America.* Bloomington: Indiana University Press, 1985.

Philip Jenkins — *Crime and Justice: Issues and Ideas.* Monterey, CA: Brooks-Cole, 1984.

Wendy Kaminer — *It's All the Rage: Crime and Culture.* Reading, MA: Addison-Wesley, 1995.

Victor E. Kappeler — *The Mythology of Crime and Criminal Justice.* Prospect Heights, IL: Waveland Press, 1996.

Burton S. Katz — *Justice Overruled: Unmasking the Criminal Justice System.* New York: Warner Books, 1997.

Randall Kennedy — *Race, Crime, and the Law.* New York: Pantheon Books, 1997.

David Luban — *Lawyers and Justice: An Ethical Study.* Princeton, NJ: Princeton University Press, 1988.

Patrick B. McGuigan and Jon S. Pascale, eds. — *Crime and Punishment in Modern America.* Lanham, MD: University Press of America, 1986.

Coramae Richey Mann — *Unequal Justice: A Question of Color.* Bloomington: Indiana University Press, 1993.

Marc Mauer — *Young Black Men and the Criminal Justice System: A Growing National Problem.* Washington, DC: The Sentencing Project, 1990.

Jerome G. Miller — *Search and Destroy: African-American Males in the Criminal Justice System.* Cambridge: Cambridge University Press, 1996.

Roslyn Muraskin, ed. — *Issues in Justice: Exploring Policy Issues in the Criminal Justice System.* Bristol, IN: Wyndham Hall Press, 1990.

Polly Nelson — *Defending the Devil: My Story as Ted Bundy's Last Lawyer.* New York: Morrow, 1994.

David Neubauer — *America's Courts and the Criminal Justice System.* Belmont, CA: Wadsworth, 1996.

Elihu Rosenblatt, ed.   *Criminal Injustice: Confronting the Prison Crisis.* Boston: South End Press, 1996.

Paula S. Rothenberg   *Race, Class, and Gender in the United States: An Integrated Study.* 2nd ed. New York: St. Martin's Press, 1992.

Harold J. Rothwax   *Guilty: The Collapse of Criminal Justice.* New York: Random House, 1996.

Edgardo Rotman   *Beyond Punishment: A New View on the Rehabilitation of Criminal Offenders.* Westport, CT: Greenwood Press, 1990.

William L. Selke   *Prisons in Crisis.* Bloomington: Indiana University Press, 1993.

Robert L. Shapiro   *The Search for Justice: A Defense Attorney's Brief on the O.J. Simpson Case.* New York: Warner Books, 1996.

David Shichor   *Three Strikes and You're Out.* Thousand Oaks, CA: Sage, 1996.

Linda Thurston, ed.   *A Call to Action: An Analysis and Overview of the United States Criminal Justice System.* Chicago: Third World Press, 1993.

Michael Tonry   *Sentencing Reform in Overcrowded Times.* New York: Oxford University Press, 1997.

Michael Tonry and Norval Morris, eds.   *Crime and Justice: A Review of Research.* Vol. 10 Chicago: University of Chicago Press, 1988.

Richard H. Uviller   *Virtual Justice: The Flawed Prosecution of Crime in America.* New Haven, CT: Yale University Press, 1996.

Eugene D. Wheeler and Robert E. Kallman   *Stop Justice Abuse.* Ventura, CA: Pathfinder Press, 1986.

William Wilbanks   *The Myth of a Racist Criminal Justice System.* Monterey, CA: Brooks-Cole, 1987.

INDEX

Abraham, Lynne, 50, 54
accused persons. *See* criminal defendants
Adams, John, 186
African Americans
  are discriminated against
    in criminal justice system, 17–20
      con, 21–24
    in police departments, 95–96
    see also poor, the
  conviction rates of, 22–24, 168–69
    for drug offenses, 19, 22
    for "three strikes" offenses, 113
  and death penalty, 22, 52–53
Alley, Sedley, 57, 58–59, 62
Alschuler, Albert, 141–42
Amar, Akhil Reed, 33
Amar, Vikram David, 33
American Bar Association, 173
  Code of Professional Conduct in, 167
appellate courts, 178–79, 190
Apperson, Jay, 122
Arenella, Peter, 86
Arnold, Thurman, 153
attorneys
  adversarial, excess of, 152–53
  changing stories of, 157–58
  as courtroom actors, 156–57, 162, 178
  defense
    and appeals courts, 190
    distort the truth, 177, 181–82, 184
      con, 188
    ethics of, 173–76, 178, 183–84
    and exclusionary rule, 190
    focus on police misconduct, 73
    have no power over judicial process, 68
    historical undermining of, 186–87
    and indigents defense, 189
    keep judicial process honest, 188–89
    lack resources of prosecutors, 47,
      160–61, 163
    and media, 169–70, 187
    and *Miranda* rule, 76, 78, 79
    myths about, 187–91
    in O.J. Simpson case, 155, 156, 158,
      175–76, 188
    provoke judicial errors, 181–82
    public defenders as, 161, 162, 163, 189
    public perception of, 46, 169
    and reasonable doubt, 181
    responsibilities of, 167, 170, 178,
      183, 186
    Robert Shapiro as, 165–71
    and "three strikes" law, 112
    and willful ignorance of guilt, 175
    workload of, 47

  discovery abuses of, 153–54
  ethics codes of, 166–67
  and expert testimonies, 158
  interpret laws, 167
  and jury selection, 34, 37, 46
  peremptory challenges of, 33, 37, 154
  presumptuous questions of, 155–56
  prosecution
    appeals insure accountability of, 178–79
    control judicial process, 68
    and death penalty, 52
    and defendant's trial rights, 164
    and exclusionary rule, 93
    have advantage over defense, 160–61,
      163
    lenient treatment by, 24
    leverage reduced by *Miranda* rule, 82
    in O.J. Simpson case, 157
    and plea bargaining, 45, 116–17
    and "probably guilty" citizens,
      180–81
    responsibilities of, 167, 178
    support minimum sentences, 123,
      124–25
    and "three strikes" law, 108, 111–12
    want clear rules, 183
    witness abuse by, 156
    witness coaching by, 154–55
    see also judges

Bascue, James, 48
Bazelon, David, 69
Bell, Larry Gene, 58, 62
Berger v. United States, 167
Bernardo, Paul, 58, 62
Bias, Len, 126
Bill of Rights. *See under* United States
Bittaker, Lawrence, 58, 60, 62
Blackmun, Harry, 55
blacks. *See* African Americans
Blackstone, William, 168
Blaming theVictim (Ryan), 72–73
"boot camp" punishment, 118, 120
Broderick, Vincent L., 114
Brown, Denise, 156
Brown, Raymond, 46
Bugliosi, Vincent, 172
Bundy, Ted, 60
Burger, Warren, 67, 91
Butler, Paul, 22

Canada
  confession rates in, 80
  death penalty in, 55
  tort system of, 91

capital punishment. *See* death penalty
Carlson, Arne, 26
Carter, Jimmy, 17
Cassell, Paul, 76
Cavanagh, David, 133
Chavez, Linda, 21, 23
church leaders, 18
civil liberties
  are protected by exclusionary rule, 94–98
    con, 91–92
Clinton, Bill, 67
cocaine, 20, 22
Cochran, Johnnie, 155, 158, 176
Cohen, Felix, 154
Cohen, Mark, 133
Collins, Jack and Trudy, 57–58
Collins, Suzanne, 57, 59
Colville, Robert, 52
Congress. *See under* United States
coroners, 44
Corrections Today, 27, 143
courts. *See* appellate courts; federal courts
crime
  laboratories, 44, 188
  rates, 44, 45, 130, 133
    age-specific factors in, 143, 144
    are decreasing, 110, 112
    are steady since 1980, 26
    cost of, 132–33
    and exclusionary rule, 92
    rose in '60s and '70s, 140
    and truth-in-sentencing policies,
      135–36
    in U.S., 133, 136–37
    in Washington State, 104
  victims of
    claimed by convicted murderers, 75
    costs for, 132–33
    restorative justice for, 48
    rights amendment for, 67
  violent
    and African Americans, 19
    age-specific factors in, 143
    and property offenses, 144
    rates of, 143–44
    and recidivism, 47–48, 129–31,
      134–35
    and "three strikes" law, 110
    and truth-in-sentencing laws,
      136–37, 142–44
  see also recidivism
criminal defendants
  commit crimes while awaiting trial,
    44–45
  expected punishment of, 135–36
  guilt of, 180–81, 184
  rate of, 178
  as "mules," 123, 124–25

overcharging of, 45
plea bargaining with, 45, 116–17
and public defenders, 47
rights of, 163–64
  are protected by Bill of Rights, 68–70,
    166
  to counsel, 162–63
  deny justice to victims, 73–75
  encourage game-playing by attorneys,
    72
  protect all citizens, 69–70
and truth-in-sentencing policies, 128,
  129, 134–36
see also attorneys, defense; criminal law;
  trials
criminality
  age-specific factors in, 113, 143, 144
  predictability of, 113
  see also prisons, populations
criminal justice system
  cost of, 19, 113, 133
  must be reformed, 43–48
    regarding death penalty, 49–55
      con, 56–62
    regarding jury system, 33–42
    regarding racial discrimination,
      17–20, 170–71
      con, 21–24
  must try cases faster, 45–46
  rights of accused in
    are guaranteed by Bill of Rights, 68–70
    deny justice to victims, 73–75
    encourage game-playing by attorneys,
      72
    protect all citizens, 69–70
  safeguards for, 24
  should focus on punishment, 29–32,
    131–32
  should focus on rehabilitation, 25–28
  women in, 19
  see also criminal defendants; criminal law;
    juries; sentencing laws; trials
criminal law
  exclusionary rule in, 74, 90
    is necessary, 94–98
    should be repealed, 92–93
  Miranda rule in
    undermines judicial process, 76–83
      con, 84–89
  resists reform, 48
  see also sentencing laws
criminal trials. *See* attorneys; juries; trials
Criminal Violence, Criminal Justice (Silberman), 69
Curry, Derrick, 125–26

Darden, Christopher, 156
Darrow, Clarence, 157
Davis, Richard Allen, 110

Davis v. United States, 86
death penalty
  and African Americans, 22, 52–53
  does not deter crime, 49, 50–51, 59
  and errors in convictions, 61
  and political campaigns, 67
  should be eliminated, 49–55
    con, 56–62
defendants. See criminal defendants
Denny, Reginald, 170
DiGenova, Joseph, 46
Dillingham, Dave, 27
discrimination. See racial discrimination
Disraeli, Benjamin, 152
district attorneys. See attorneys,
  prosecution
DNA testing, 158, 168
Dole, Bob, 67
Douglas, John, 56
Dripps, Donald A., 88
drug offenses, 19, 20, 22
  and mandatory sentencing, 115–16,
    122–27
Du Bois, W.E.B., 22
du Pont, Pete, 31

Economist magazine, 38
Ehrlich, Isaac, 135
Ernest, "Sincere," 123–24
exclusionary rule, 46, 74, 77, 90
  develops Fourth Amendment, 96–97
  good-faith exemption to, 91–92, 93
  is necessary, 94–98
  should be repealed, 90–93

FBI index of crimes, 81
federal courts
  and death penalty, 53–54
  exclusionary rule in, 67, 91–92
  mandatory sentencing in, 119, 124–27
  "three strikes" law in, 110
  truth-in-sentencing policies in, 139, 146
Federalist, The, 119
Federal Sentencing Guidelines, 119
  departures from, 120
felony charges, 44
  and "three strikes" law, 20, 103–108, 110
  types of, 22
Fine, Ralph Adam, 31
Fingerprint Identification System,
  Automated, 44
Frank, Jerome, 152–53
Frankel, Marvin, 153, 180, 182
Franklin, Daniel, 111
Franks, Bobby, 60
Freedman, Monroe, 183–84
Friendly, Henry, 74
From Bondage (Roth), 176

Fuhrman, Mark, 72

Galsworthy, John, 67
Garcetti, Gil, 52
Germany, Nazi, 186
Gest, Ted, 43
Gideon v. Wainwright, 162–63
Gordon, Steven Drake, 111
Gramm, Phil, 125
Grano, Joseph D., 46, 175
Great Britain
  confession rates in, 80
  death penalty in, 55
Greer, William, 132
Grego, Jim, 48
Griffin, Dwight Anthony, 106–107
Guilty: The Collapse of Criminal Justice
  (Rothwax), 81, 92, 155, 177

Hamilton, Alexander, 119
Harlan, John Marshall, 82
Harris, Robert Alton, 72
Harvard Journal of Law and Public Policy, 86, 97,
  175
Henkel, Heinrich, 186
Heymann, Philip, 123
Hispanics
  in criminal justice system, 19
  and "three strikes" law, 113
Holmes, Johnny, 52
Holmes, Oliver Wendell, Jr., 118
Huling, Tracey, 19

incarceration. See prisons
inmates. See prisons, populations

Jacobs, Jesse, 50
jails. See prisons
Jeffrey, Douglas, 132
Johnson, Michael Elton, 104–105
Johnson, Robert, 52
Jordan, James, 136
Journey into Darkness (Douglas), 56
judges
  and exclusionary rule, 97
  and Federal Sentencing Guidelines,
    119–20
  as guardians of justice, 69
  and indeterminate sentencing, 141
  jury instruction by, 168
  and mandatory minumum sentencing
    laws, 115, 117, 118
  and prison release policies, 141
  questionable ethics of, 154
  responsibility of, 182–83
  and "three strikes" law, 110, 112
  trial-management training for, 46
juries

and black conviction rates, 22, 23–24
and court professionals, 36, 37, 39–40,
   168
need reform, 36–41, 46
nullification by, 22, 24, 113
and presumption of innocence, 181
and presumptuous questions, 155–56
and reasonable doubt, 168
selection process of, 34, 37, 46
as self-government, 35, 36, 39
service on, avoided by citizens, 34, 38
and sympathy factor, 116
see also Simpson trial
Justice Department. See under United States

Kemper, Ed, 60
King, Rodney, 72, 96, 170
Klaas, Polly, 110, 113, 136
Kleiman, Mark, 133
Klein, Susan R., 84

LaCourse, David, Jr., 103
law enforcement. See police departments
lawyers. See attorneys
legal services, 163
Leopold, Nathan, 60
Lerner, Robert, 21, 23
Lewis, Angela, 123–24, 125, 126, 127
life imprisonment. See death penalty;
   sentencing laws, "three strikes"
Lincoln, Abraham, 186
Llewellyn, Karl, 152
Loeb, Richard, 60
Logan, Charles H., 29
Los Angeles Times, 188
Lungren, Daniel, 71

MacDonald, Jeffrey, 174–75
MacDougall, Ellis, 18
Mahoney, Barry, 46
mandatory minimum sentencing laws,
   114, 124, 190–91
and drug dealers, 122–27
numerical crime factors in, 118
plea bargaining in, 116–18
in political campaigns, 67
and prison overcrowding, 116
should be abolished, 114–21
Manson, Charles, 173
Mapp v. Ohio, 74, 91, 95
Mardigian, Steve, 58
Markman, Stephen J., 76
Martinez, Anne, 69
Mauer, Marc, 19, 138
McCloskey, James, 49
McNamara, Joseph D., 109
medical examiners, 44
Medical Marijuana Act. See Proposition 215

Milk, Harvey, 175
minimum sentencing. See mandatory
   minimum sentencing laws
minorities. See African Americans;
   Hispanics; racial discrimination
Miranda rule, 68
amends Constitution, 78
hampers successful prosecution, 76,
   81–82
lowers confession rates, 79–81
con, 88
no remedies for violation of, 85, 87–88
should be replaced, 81, 82–83
should be strengthened, 88–89
Miranda v. Arizona, 77–79
Montesquieu, Baron, 93
Moran v. Burbine, 85
Moscone, George, 175

National Center for Policy Analysis, 135
National Center for State Courts, 45–46
National Criminal Victims Survey, 134
National Institute of Justice, 82
National Research Council, 144
New York Times, 51
New York Times Magazine, 52
Nunn, Kenneth B., 159

Orfi, Alan, 25, 163
Outrage: The Five Reasons Why O.J. Simpson Got
   Away with Murder (Bugliosi), 172

parole, 48
as failed experiment, 137
in indeterminate sentencing, 141
see also recidivism
Parole Board, U.S., 131
Partisan Justice (Frankel), 180
peremptory strikes, 33, 37
Perspective (periodical), 26
Philadelphia Inquirer, 50–51
plea bargaining, 142
bans on, 45
and mandatory minimum sentencing
   laws, 116–18
police departments
and defense attorneys, 188
and exclusionary rule, 74, 90–98, 190
legal liability of, 92
lose vital evidence, 44
and Miranda rule, 68, 76–80, 82–83
violations of, 85–88
misconduct in, 72–73, 82–83, 93, 96
need more manpower, 44
and racial discrimination, 95–96
use of videotaping in, 82
politicians
and defense attorneys, 186

and mandatory sentences, 114, 115, 119
and truth-in-sentencing laws, 139
use crime as campaign theme, 17, 19,
    26, 67, 190–91
poor, the
and criminal justice system, 17–18
and jury duty, 37
and police departments, 95–96
Powell, Lewis, 55
Prince, Cleophus, 61–62
Prison Mirror, 25, 163
prisons
cost of, 113, 133, 136
    life sentences, 51
"get tough" policies in, 26–28
increased need for, 48, 112, 133–34
must punish, 29–32
must rehabilitate, 19, 20, 27–28
parole boards in, 141
populations, 45
    and drug offenses, 19, 20, 22
    federal, 146
    health care for, 112
    and indeterminate sentencing, 141
    lawsuits of, 75
    "mules" in, 125
    need punishment, 29–32
        con, 27
    need rehabilitation, 25, 27–28
        con, 30–31
    nonviolent offenders in, 118, 129
    and parole, 48, 141
    research on criminal behavior in, 60
    revolts in, 20
    and "three strikes" law, 111, 112
    women in, 19
    see also recidivism
privatization of, 31–32
reforms of, 18–19
and truth-in-sentencing policies, 134,
    136, 140, 144
Private Prisons: Cons and Pros (Logan), 29
property offenses, 144
Proposition 184, 110
Proposition 215, 113
public defenders. *See under* attorneys,
    defense

racial discrimination
needs to be eliminated from criminal
    justice system, 17–20
        con, 21–24
in police departments, 95–96
Reader's Digest, 24
Rebovich, Donald, 48
recidivism, 47–48, 129–31
    and "get tough" policies, 25, 27–28
    and U.S. Parole Board, 131

Reconstructing Justice: An Agenda for Trial Reform
    (Strier), 151
Regnery, Alfred, 134–35
rehabilitation
    should be focus of criminal justice, 25–28
        con, 30–31, 131–32
religious leaders, 18
Reno, Janet, 126
Reynolds, Morgan O., 90, 135–36
Rosenberg executions, 53–54
Roth, Henry, 176
Rothwax, Harold J., 68, 81, 92, 155, 177
Ryan, Nancy, 179
Ryan, William, 72–73

Sack, Alfons, 186
Safe Street Alliance, 142
Salient Factor Score (SFS), 131
Schulhofer, Stephen, 86
Scottsboro boys, 96
Search for Justice: A Defense Attorney's Brief on the
    O.J. Simpson Case (Shapiro), 165
Sentencing Accountability Commission
    (Delaware), 145
sentencing laws, 31, 142
    mandatory minimum
        drug dealers and, 122–27
        numerical crime factors in, 118
        plea bargaining in, 116–18
    and prison release policies, 141
    public dissatisfaction with, 140
    "three strikes"
        are inconsistent and punitive, 111–12
        in California, 110-13
        change criminal behavior, 106–107
        have lowered crime rates, 106–108, 112
            con, 112–13
        and nonviolent offenses, 110–11, 113
        slow the justice system, 48, 169
        target career criminals, 107–108
        in Washington State, 103–108
    and truth-in-sentencing
        and age-specific crime factors, 144
        in Delaware, 144
        federal adoption of, 139, 146
        and federal aid for prisons, 139
        and state sentencing policies, 142
        states should adopt, 128–37
        states should have clear goals for,
            139–47
Sentencing Project, The, 19
Sevilla, Charles M., 185
Shandel, Martin T., 105
Shapiro, Robert L., 158, 165
Shilling, Bob, 107
Shipp, Ron, 156
Silberman, Charles, 69
Simpson, Nicole Brown, 156

Simpson trial
  Bugliosi on, 173, 175–76
  changing story in, 158
  defense attorneys' role in, 46–47, 188
  jury in, 46
  peremptory challenges in, 154
  Shapiro on, 166, 170–71
  witness coaching in, 155
Smith, Adam, 73
Sperlich, Peter, 158
Stalder, Richard, 142
State Backgrounder (periodical), 129
Steiker, Carol S., 94
Stein, Gertrude, 176
Stone, Harlan, 119
Strier, Franklin, 151
Stuntz, William J., 97
Supreme Court. *See under* United States
Symbols of Government, The (Arnold), 153

Tate-LaBianca murders, 173
Tocqueville, Alexis de, 35
"three strikes" policies. *See under* sentencing
  laws
trials, 180
  are too adversarial, 151–58
    con, 159–64
  length of time for, 45–46
  and "third-strike" offenses, 48
  see also judges; Simpson trial
truth-in-sentencing policies. *See under*
  sentencing laws
Twin Cities Reader, 28

United States
  attorney general, 54, 126
  Bill of Rights
    and citizen juries, 34, 35
    Eighth Amendment, 120, 166
    Fifth Amendment, 77, 78, 88, 166
    Fourth Amendment, 74, 90–98, 166
    and modern crime, 168
    and rights of accused, 68–79
    Seventh Amendment, 166
    Sixth Amendment, 162–63, 166, 186,
      187
  Congress, 77
    on crack cocaine laws, 20
    and exclusionary rule, 46, 67, 91–92
    and federal funding for defense, 47
    and mandatory minumum sentencing
      laws, 116, 119, 125
    and "three strikes" law, 110
    truth-in-sentencing policies of, 146
  Constitution, 179, 187
    amended by *Miranda* rule, 68
    Article 3 of, 119–20

  see also United States, Bill of Rights
  Justice Department
    Bureau of Justice Statistics, 22, 23,
      129, 130
      on repeat offenders, 82
    on death penalty, 53, 55
    habitual offender program of, 134–35
    victimization surveys by, 144
  Parole Board, 131
  Supreme Court
    on the death penalty, 52, 53, 55
    on defendant's right to counsel,
      162–63
    on exclusionary rule, 74, 91, 95, 96–97
    on *Miranda* rule, 77–80
    on prosecutors, 167
    on "separate but equal" laws, 18
    on trials, 152
    see also Warren Court
  United States v. Angela Lewis & "Sincere" Ernest,
    123–24
  United States v. Leon, 74
  USA Today, 69
  U.S. News & World Report, 44, 45

Vasquez, David, 61

Wachtler, Sol, 66
Wall Street Journal, 23
Walton, Reggie B., 24
Warren Court, 68
  and exclusionary rule, 90–93
  and the *Miranda* rule, 76, 83
Washington Monthly, 111
Washington Post, 125–26
Washington Times, 31, 125
Webster, Daniel, 186
Weeks v. United States, 74, 91
Weitzman, Howard, 188
White, Byron, 78, 83
White, Dan, 175
white Americans
  as cocaine dealers, 22
  conviction rates of, 22–24
  see also poor, the
Whitman, Walt, 120
Wilkey, Malcolm, 93
Wilson, James Q., 131–32
Wilson, Pete, 111
Wolfgang, Marvin, 125, 134
Wootton, James, 6, 128, 142–44

Yale Law Journal, 22

Zedlewski, Edward W., 133
Zobel, Hiller B., 38